The Pen & the Sword

The struggle of Hispaniola's Media

Volume One

Bernard Diederich

Dedication

In 1977 disaster stuck Jean Desquiron. He lost his beloved wife to cancer and his youngest daughter to an automobile accident. In an effort to draw my brother-in-law and close friend out of depression I suggested we write about the media together even though the subject could be dangerous and depressing. We started this book and then shelved it when he decided to write his series., "Haiti a La Une". This first volume is dedicated to Jean, may he rest in peace.

isbn

Cover designed by Jean Bernard Diederich

Paintings in the book are by Emmanuel Saincilus
Ancient photos are from the archives of CIDIHCA.

Chapters

Introduction

Introduction

The Admiral returns to the sea.

　　To commemorate Port-au-Prince's bicentennial, Spain sent a gift, a large statue of the "Admiral of the Ocean Sea". For 36 years Christopher Columbus knelt at the land's end of Port-au-Prince tourist jetty. His well rounded behind welcomed disembarking cruise ship visitors, in the 1950s.

　　On the other hand the sculpture of the tall muscular man, who discovered the island in 1492, acted as a magnet for couples who parked their automobile on Harry Truman blvd in the cool of the evening and many a lover stared into the Admiral's large dark molded steel eyes.

　　With the end of the long Duvalier Dictatorship, when dechoukaj was all the rage, strong men, led by a history buff, heaved Columbus into the ocean. When it was noted that the admiral was back in the sea, the city returned him to his pedestal only to have the *dechoukaj* team heave him back into the ocean again. Finally the city fathers had enough and parked Columbus out of sight under the Hotel de Ville where he was last seen when the building collapsed during the 2010 earthquake that devastated the city. In 2016 the Minister of Culture, Marc Garcia, suggested that as Môle Saint Nicolas, celebrated and with gusto, December 5, the date of discovery, the statue belonged there.

The Admiral in Port-au-Prince.

"History is a river of truth which flows majestically through the ages…History is the echo of human storms, whose clamor and fury it faithfully reproduces…"

From Stella: by Emeric Bergeaud, the first novel by a Haitian, published in Paris in 1859.

Chapter 1

With Discovery Came Genocide

The ebb and flow of Hispaniola's early history has been largely chronicled by its visitors and for that reason the island's history has been difficult to trace from the outset, obscured by the lack of accurate information and biases of those who recorded it. First among them were the early explorers, beginning with Christopher Columbus and the Spanish theologians who accompanied them. Historians have had to pick their way carefully through the trail of journals, letters, dispatches and even ships' logs to fit together the puzzle of history in their attempt to separate fact from fiction. Some of the earliest records of this tropical island were often written more to please a patron than to record the truth. Frequently legends became fact.

The Taino who inhabited the island had no written language and the early Spanish invaders were less concerned with learning the oral history of the natives than working them to death in their search for gold. The Indians had achieved a high level of development and Columbus did show interest and requested that a Spanish priest, Ramón Pané, make a study of the Taino and report back on their customs, beliefs, and way of life, which he did in 1496 before returning to Spain.

This is artist Emmanuel Saincilus rending of Christophe Columbus arrival and illustrates how he stirred the island in a cauldron to the boil to squeeze every ounce of gold out of Hispaniola.

(The Ancient Taíno people left behind beautiful petroglyphs giving an insight into their past lives and culture. They made drawings and carvings on rocks near rivers or in caves.) Still, the Spanish conquerors became the first correspondents in Hispaniola. Their journals and letters provided the first glimpses of a beautiful land of idyllic beaches and rain forests nestled among the clouds. It was they who disseminated the news in chronicle form of their voyages resulting in the conquest of the New World.

Along with the men of the sword, came men of the cross, better prepared as writers. They were followed by traveler-diplomats, or a special envoy. From their reports came the first knowledge of Hispaniola. Christopher Columbus, who penned a Journal of his initial visit in 1492, was the first reporter. He named the island Hispaniola, after Spain, for whom he sailed. The original Journal of that First Voyage was lost, but copies were made, which contain not only the trip's first log but information about the people, fauna and flora and views on its colonization.

The Chinese had made early advances in printing with movable type and in 1454 the Gutenberg bible was printed, and, before the 15th century was over, print shops had appeared in Spain.

The Taino society had existed on the island for several thousand years when the Europeans arrived to terminate their existence with forced work in gold mines, the swords, fire and diseases for which they had no immunity.

Fray Bartolomé de Las Casas, of the Dominican order, who became known as the "Apostle of the Indians," in effect was the first "whistle-blowing" reporter of the period. He arrived in Hispaniola in 1502; the year a hurricane destroyed Santo Domingo, to become a priest on the island. It was after the murderous pacification of Cuba he ended up in Chiapas, in south Mexico where he was made bishop. In 1514, twelve years into witnessing the conquest, he had an awakening and saw the genocide committed by fellow Spaniards on the Indian.

Las Casas made Chiapas a holy city before returning to Spain in 1547, and he accused the Conquistadors of genocide against the native Indian populations. His exposé, *Brevisima Relacion de la Destruccion de las Indias*, was not published in Spain printed until 1575 and it became an instant best-seller in Europe. When he learned of the treatment of the African slaves on Hispaniola, Las Casas repented that he had suggested they be imported from Africa to provide the new work force. More blood soaked the soil of the island. (Descendant of Indians who managed to survive took the names of birds.)

Las Casas kept writing until he died at 92, however he was not the first to protest the treatment of the Indians--"dirty dogs" the Spaniards called them--. In 1511 Dominican friar Antonio de Montesinos cried out from his Santo Domingo pulpit to his Spanish congregation against their treatment of the Indians telling them they were in mortal sin.

"You live and die in mortal sin, for the cruelty and tyranny you use in dealing with these innocent people. Tell me, by what right or justice do you keep these Indians in such a cruel and horrible servitude...For with the excessive work you demand of them they fall ill and die, or rather you kill them with your desire to extract and acquire gold every day..."

Chapter 2

Indians treated as Dogs

Hispaniola became the first killing fields of the New World. The brutality and madness of the conquest decimated the island population, originally estimated at 800,000 to one million. By 1548, Spanish historian Gonzalo Fernandez de Valdes Oviedo estimated their numbers at less than 500.

Columbus' son, Ferdinand (Don Hernando Colon), became another of the early chroniclers of Hispaniola and what might be considered its first "intellectual." A book lover who made the fourth trip to the New World with his father, he assembled one of the early libraries of Hispaniola. He took it with him when he returned to Spain. Other early "reporters" were Fernandez de Oviedo y Valdes, Pietro Martyr d'Anghiera and Girolamo Benzoni, who published *La Historia del Mondo Novo* in 1865.

Gold was the early magnet that drew the Spaniards to Hispaniola, where they established a number of towns in both the west, now Haiti, and the east, now the Dominican Republic. When the gold ran out, many headed for Mexico and Peru. Hispaniola stagnated, becoming a way station en route to richer lands on the Spanish Main.

Was it all this bloodshed that fertilized tyrannies that were to bloom with the same profusion as the island's tropical flowers? Freedom of speech was to remain a delicate plant. For most of its history it remained an odious scent to the island's autocratic leaders into the 21st century.

Nicolás de Ovando became the island's governor in 1502 and brought the first black Christianized slaves from Spain to Hispaniola. Ovando is the one who went west into what is today Haiti. There were Spaniard, "renegades" they were called, living with the Indians. Xaragua as it was called was the last prehispanic holdout on the island. It was the realm of Anacaona. She greeted Ovando and his troops. He selected the. Eighty caciques who had been invited to meet the governor along with their paramount chief, into a canery which the governor ordered torched and they were burned alive. Anacaona was hung.

Nearly a century later a different "golden age" dawned in the Caribbean. Writers, poets and dramatists were stirred to action by the region's romance and intrigue. At the same time, the struggle for control between Spain and France began in the newly drawn map of the Caribbean Sea and the Spanish Main beyond. That, too, attracted attention.

Built during the regime of Jean-Claude Duvalier as a tribute to the Indians it was later destroyed. (Photo by the author)

The Virgin of the Navigators by Alego Fernandez in 1531 is the earliest known painting of the discovery of the Americas. The reproduction is by Emmanuel Saincilus. The barque implanted at the Right hand corner is of the Pamir.

Chapter 3

Sir Francis Drake sailed and plundered

German Arciniegas, in his 1946 work, "*Caribbean Sea Of The New World*," took note of the period:

"Rabelais wrote the fantastic voyages of Pantagruel, perhaps the most magnificent of his books, inspired by the voyages of the pirate Juan Florentin. Cervantes could not make up his mind whether to write *Don Quixote* or sail for the Caribbean, to Guatemala, to the kingdom of New Granada – a refuge, as he himself says, for rogues and thieves. Shakespeare filled his dramas with scenes taken from Raleigh's trips to Guiana. Lope de Vega composes his *Dragontea* on the life of Francis Drake, whom the Spanish called the Dragon and worse. If one drew a literary map of the Caribbean, there would be found on it all the names of the poets, novelists, the dramatist's, as though they had dreamed of setting their republic of letters alongside the tents of the buccaneers or the watch fire of the freebooters."

They all contributed to the evolution of the traveler as historian and foreign correspondent.

The buccaneers moved to the mainland of Hispaniola from La Tortue, their island lair off the north coast. In this mountainous Western region the French eventually settled.

Hispaniola, as the other Caribbean islands, became a jewel in the crowns of Europe and their navies fought important sea battles for them. It was not unusual for the French and Spanish or the French and English to end up sharing the same island over which they fought, more often than not over sugar. In 1697, Spain ceded the western third of Hispaniola – an area that boasted more French than Spanish speaking settlers – to the French in the treaty of Ryswick.

The famous British navigator, pirate to the New World, Sir Francis Drake published, in 1653, a summary of his voyages to the West Indies. But he won no praise from Hispaniola, just criticism for his heretic ways--stabling the horses in the ancient cathedral of Santo Domingo.

The tethering rings are still there. It must be remembered that this famous sailor was then fighting their Catholic majesties, England having broken with the Church of Rome.

"Since the assault of Drake and his English rogues
Your neglected walls have crumbled in decay
And like a glorious necklace of black pearls
Display the gaping rents torn by de Point . . ."
Jose María de Heredia (A Cartagena.)

An ancient map of Santo Domingo and the Ozama river.

Saint-Domingue and San Domingo

Saint Domingue, as the French part became known, developed with the import of African Slaves. It also received greater attention abroad than the Spanish part or Hispaniola.

Moreau de Saint Mery, a lawyer and writer, was perhaps the most famous 18th Century reporter/Chronicler, who, besides his work on the French side, also published two volumes on the Spanish portion in 1796. The standard work on early San Domingo is a four-volume set entitled "*Histoire de l'Isle ou de Saint-Domingue,*" by Father C.F.X Charlevoix in Amsterdam in 1733. It relied heavily on the memoirs of Father Jean-Baptiste Le Pons, a Jesuit missionary in Hispaniola.

12

Chapter 4

Island's first Journalist-Publisher

The first journalist on Saint-Domingue had an inauspicious beginning on an island subject to even more severe restrictions than those existing today. His name, Joseph Payen, a native of France and printer by trade. He arrived in 1724, opening a bookshop in Cap François (now Cap Haitien) and announcing his intention to publish a newspaper. It was news that alarmed the governor of the colony, De Rochalard. A violent rebellion had only recently been put down and De Rochalard saw a newspaper adding a disturbing element to the situation. He ordered the arrest of Payen, charging him with selling pornographic material.

Payen was released after presenting his royal patent letters as a printer to the governor, who angrily tore them up. When Payen eventually began publication of his newspaper – the name of which there is no record – he was again jailed and then shipped back to France along with his printing press. It was an ominous beginning that appeared to set a trend lasting through contemporary times. The account of Payen was recorded in 1993 in "*Haiti a La Une*" by Jean Desquiron, who spent years painstakingly examining the press in Saint-Domingue and Haiti, which it later became.

Rayford W. Logan, in his 1968 study, "*Haiti and The Dominican Republic*," states that "the first publication from a printing press appeared at Leogane [Haiti] on 1725," adding that it was the only recorded publication until the 1760's. Logan also notes that "the period of French rule coincided more or less with the Age of Enlightenment and the colony was closely in touch with the intellectual life of the home country. Several books about it by Frenchmen who lived there for varying periods of time were published in France. An early resident, Father Pierre Boudin, S.J., who arrived at Cap-Français in 1714, taught blacks and studied astronomy and African dialects until his death in 1742.

Saint-Domingue, unlike Spanish Santo Domingo, had no university and its few schools provided only an elementary education. The privileged few sought their higher education in France. But as Logan notes, "nothing comparable occurred in Santo Domingo. People in the Spanish colony were far less in touch with contemporary Europe, and in any case the Spanish Age of Enlightenment lacked the scope and intensity of the French. A printing press existed, but no work concerning the administration might be published without permission from the Spanish Council of the Indies.

"The University of St. Thomas Aquinas, founded in Santo Domingo in 1558, appears to have had fewer distinguished scholars and students than the Universities of Mexico, San Marcos in Lima, or even of Cordoba in the interior of Argentina. The white Creoles were not well educated and most of the country people were completely illiterate. Moreau de St. Mery acknowledges, however, his indebtedness to two notable writers, Alfonso de Espinosa and Antonio Valverde. Even in the capital the only theatrical performances were occasional farces and comedies. Bullfighting provided the principal amusement."

It wasn't until Feb. 1, 1764 that Saint Domingue saw a regular newspaper. *La Gazete de Saint Domingue*, founded by Antoine Marie, was more of a business paper, with emphasis on classified advertisements rather than news items. The Gazette kept its readers informed on French commerce by reprinting information published on business, agriculture and navigation as well as cultural affairs. It advertised properties for sale and rent and the price of commodities along with freight and shipping rates. Although there was nothing subversive in the Gazette's advertisements and reprinted articles from France the French Royal government ordered it closed.

Admiral Comte D'Estaing, who was then the governor (1774-76) of Saint Domingue, made it known that the newspaper's title, made it sound too much like an official paper, not the content, that bothered him. He suggested Antoine Marie find a more innocuous name, which he did. Thus was born *Avis Divers et Petites Affiches Americaines*, soon to be known simply as *Affiches Americaines*. By 1788, the newspaper had 1,500 subscribers.

A typical classified ad in the *Affiches Americaines* of the day: "A nice chaise for three passengers, painted yellow in the middle of raw panels, large gilt edges, garnished with Utrecht velours, double curtains with springs, and of which the shafts and wheels are made in the colony, and further the harness for four horses."

Some were typical of the colony: "For sale: a distillery located at Leogane with four wagons, 12 mules, 30 blacks and other utensils necessary to the distillery," or: For sale: Some furniture, chairs, beds, 3 domestic blacks and other objects."

They appeared as part of the boom years that began in 1740. By 1798, Saint-Domingue accounted for half of France's foreign trade. There were about 400,000 African slaves, half of whom had been born on the island; 40,000 whites and some 28,000 mulattos.

Concern about slavery was rarely voiced. The exception was Abbe Raynol, whose "*Histoire des deux Indies*" had an impact on abolition. .

Chapter 5

News of the French Revolution

The French Revolution brought change in Saint Domingue. The classified ads were soon replaced by the fiery articles of Gatineau in *"LAmi de L'Egalite"* and Gaterau in *"Le Courrier Politique Et Litterarie"*. The revolutionary ideal of the *"Rights of Man"* crossed the Atlantic. So upsetting were Gatineau and Gaterau's articles that a member of the Colonial Assembly asked that "the liberty of the press be suppressed for having caused the ruin of Saint Domingue. The colony was flourishing; but since it [the press] has been allowed to write on all kinds of subjects, tranquility and wealth have disappeared. Rather than admit the liberty of the press, it would be more advisable to do like that emperor of China who burned the presses, the books and the writers."

The French Revolution had become a major world story and it taxed the few foreign correspondents in the field to the point that *"The Times of London"* had to advertise for more "agents,' as correspondents were then known. The following advertisement appeared in the newspaper on Aug. 27, 1792.

"Wanted immediately, a gentleman who is capable of translating the French language. In order to prevent trouble, he must be a perfect Master of the English language, have some knowledge of the Political State of Europe and be thoroughly capable of the Situation he undertakes. His employment will be permanent and take up considerable share of his Attention; for which a handsome Salary will be allowed. Apply at the office of this Paper between hours of Five and Six this evening or tomorrow Morning between Eleven and twelve O'clock."

The French Revolution was a big story as well in Saint-Domingue where the *"Rights of Man"* had an unsettling ring for the rich landowners. Newspapers and pamphlets from France helped kindle the fires of revolt among the slaves. Their uprising was to be one of the longest running major stories at the end of the 18th century. It began in August 1791, leading eventually to Haiti's independence in 1804.

Although no foreign correspondents were dispatched to cover the slave rebellion 600 miles from the shores of America, it did attract avid interest abroad. There were credible fears that the revolt might spill over into the United States as well as other Caribbean colonies. That fear accelerated as the royalists, the colonialists and then Napoleon's Veteran soldiers proved no match for the former slaves.

While the revolt attracted no foreign correspondents as such, it did have its chroniclers. "Fortunately for historical accuracy," wrote H.P. Davis in his 1928 book, *Black Democracy*, "Bryan Edwards, distinguished British historian, who arrived at Cap Francais shortly after the initial revolt and while the Northern plain was still in flames, had left a first-hand account…"

According to Edwards, "it is attested that, within two months after the revolt began, upwards of two thousand whites had been massacred, one hundred and eighty sugar plantations and about nine hundred coffee, cotton, and indigo settlements had been destroyed (the buildings had been destroyed by fire); and twelve hundred families reduced from opulence to abject destitution. Of the insurgents, it was said that upwards of ten thousand had perished by the sword or famine and some hundreds by the hand of the executioner, many of these on the wheel."

Controversy over "Bois Caiman "continues even today as to whether it happened that night in August 1791. Foreign evangelists have their own religious version of Bois Caiman which they use as a tool in fighting Vodou. They wrongly declare that at Bois Caiman the vodou practitioners made a pact with the devil that had no time limit. Following King Henry Christophe's death, the country was united, Hérard Dumesle, a mulatto writer from Aux Cayes, decided to take a look at the former kingdom. While in the North, fascinated by stories written, by Frenchmen about the launching of the slave revolt in 1791, he decided to search for the place where the slave leader had ignited the revolt in the north. From interviews he learned that at the religious ceremony a bull, not a pig, had been sacrificed but little more. Unlike others he did not cite Boukman, who some state was a Muslim and led the ceremony, sacrificing a Toro, certainly not a pig, as the gathering feasted on the meat of the sacrificed animal. Frustrated, Dumesle wrote a poem about the slaves that night in 1791, calling on God's, (Bondye,) help in overcoming the white slave masters who worshipped another God. Dumesle's account was published in 1824 on the government presses. (See Asson & the Cross (2014) Henri Deschamps.)

Chapter 6

Slave Uprising in 1791

The revolution in Saint Domingue unleashed a massive multiracial exodus: the French fled with the bonds people they managed to keep; so did numerous free people of color, some of whom were slaveholders themselves. In addition, in 1793, a catastrophic fire destroyed two-thirds of the principal city, Cap Français, and nearly ten thousand people left the island for good. In the ensuing decades of revolution, foreign invasion, and civil war, thousands more fled the turmoil. Many moved eastward to Santo Domingo (present-day Dominican Republic) or to nearby Caribbean islands. Large numbers of immigrants, black and white, found shelter in North America, notably in New York, Baltimore (fifty-three ships landed there in July 1793), Philadelphia, Norfolk, Charleston, and Savannah, as well as in Spanish Florida. Nowhere on the continent, however, did the refugee movement exert as profound an influence as in southern Louisiana.

In 1698, French explorer Sieur d'Iberville had left Saint Domingue to establish a settlement at Biloxi, on the Gulf Coast of Louisiana. A trickle of black migrants followed. However, between the 1790s and 1809, large numbers of Haitians of African descent migrated to Louisiana. By 1791 the Haitian Revolution had begun and the thousands of refugees from the fighting had profound repercussions on Louisiana's politics, the culture, the religion, and the racial climate of the state.

(The Kingdom of France controlled the Louisiana territory from 1699 until it was ceded to Spain in 1762. Napoleon in 1800, dreaming of a North American empire, regained ownership of Louisiana. The future emperor Napoleon Bonaparte's dream fizzled in 1803 because his disastrous expedition against Toussaint L'Ouverture and war with Britain had bankrupted his finances and his once powerful Army and he sold the vast North American territory known as the "Louisiana Purchase.")

Eastern Seaboard newspapers in the United States as well as Louisiana hungered for news from Saint-Domingue, with seaports in many of these cities had close ties with the

Caribbean. In addition, some French colonialists, who had sought refuge in East Coast U.S. towns after the initial slave uprising in 1791, had started their own French "exile" newspapers. Published reports appearing in these U.S. newspapers purporting to reflect events in Saint Domingue relied heavily on letters and official correspondence. Many of the newspapers of the period, which provided a primary source of information for historians about the slave rebellion, have long since disappeared. (See index)

Soldiers, diplomats and shipping agents offered rare first hand glimpses of Saint-Domingue at war. One such was Lieutenant Thomas Phipps Howard assigned to Saint Domingue with a York Hussars regiment as part of the British invasion force. Howard kept a journal of events, publishing it on his return to Britain. His account is among the best on the British invasion of 1793-98 and its crushing defeat by Toussaint Louverture. Toussaint fascinated the world at the time as no other leader apart from Napoleon. More than a dozen books were written dealing with Toussaint's rise from slavery to fight the French, English and Spanish, and his eventual betrayal.

The Spanish turned Santo Domingo over to the French in 1795 under the Treaty of Basel, as Toussaint was establishing his rule over Saint Domingue. On Jan. 26, 1801, Toussaint entered Santo Domingo and declared slavery abolished. He then defeated a British expeditionary force before battling Napoleon's best troops who landed in 1802 to reestablish French rule and slavery. Toussaint was tricked and taken to prison in France where he died in a dungeon, at Fort de Joux April 7, 1803 that is now called Chateau de Joux.

No other leader, apart from Napoleon, at that time, fascinated the world as did Toussaint. More than a dozen books were written dealing with Toussaint's rise from slavery to fight the French, English and Spanish, and his eventual betrayal and death. In fact one the biography on his life is titled, "*The Black Napoleon*," published in 1931 by Percy Waxman.

Ralph Korngold in his 1944 book, *Citizen Toussaint* notes, "With the exception of Pauleus Sannon, (*La Guerre de l'Independence*, Port-au-Prince 1925) the biographers of Toussaint have done scant justice to the subject. They are sketchy, inaccurate and for the most part represent the protagonist either as a spotless saint or an unmitigated scoundrel. Some--heedless of Henry Adams' warning to historians, " The Historian must not try to know what is truth, if he values his honesty; for if he cares for his truth, he is certain to falsify the facts"--view history through the distorting spectacle of a social philosophy.

The author notes, "The only biography of Toussaint of value to the student is that of Pauleus Sannon, who, however, has confined himself to a recital of the facts, without attempting interpretation. Yet without such interpretation the facts seem truly bewildering. He has moreover overlooked some important sources of information, as for example the entire Stevens-Pickering correspondence. (Edward Stevens, was the American Consul-General in St. Domingue at the time (1798-1800) and his dispatches to Timothy Pickering U.S. Secretary of State are important.)

Tricked and kidnapped in Haiti on Napoleon's orders and placed in a fortress-prison on a Jura mountain top 1n 1802.Here are recent photographs by Michael Tarr and his comment:

Fort de Joux where on this fidget mountain top Napoleon imprisoned Toussaint to die.

"This brought tears to my eyes and a lump to my throat. Even the most impervious to guilt about European wickedness to black men would flinch at the sight of this cell. All admirers of the great Napoleon should come here and see what he did to Haiti's Mandela and remember that he tried to re impose slavery on Haiti." Michael Tarr.

The tough, give-no-quarter, General Jean-Jacques Dessalines, was left to defeat the French troops. On Jan. 1, 1804, Dessalines and his victorious generals proclaimed Haiti's independence. It followed the United States as the second republic in the Western Hemisphere, and the world's first black nation.

Chapter 7

Journalists; Unimportant

Haiti's post-colonial leaders viewed newspapers as little more than a means to publish government decrees and official acts, as in the colony. Reporters were not essential, a tradition that continued through much of Haiti's history. The only need was for writers, people who could put words together and read proof. Newspapers were as rudimentary as the art of printing. The early writers were more politicians than journalists. They had their own agendas and little knowledge or understanding of even the most basic journalistic ethics and professional integrity.

The journalistic rules remained much the same, whether under the colonial governments, post-colonial governments or American Occupation Forces in the early 20th century: say what you want, but do not criticize or embarrass the government. President Nord Alexis (1902-08) put it more crudely: "I know that grammar is the art of writing and speaking; try to write and speak and you will see what will happen." Writers were little more than sycophants. An opposition press was not tolerated, and, even when it was, it was mediocre and unreliable. From the beginning, however, there were valiant exceptions that had to face exile and even death for their nonconformity, or for reporting something the government did not want to hear.

In a barely literate nation, Dessalines, established the new nations' first newspaper, *Gazette Politique Et Commercial d'Haiti* (1804-1807). There had been no reporters or agents accompanying Dessalines and Henry Christophe to record in detail their 1803 invasion of the eastern side of the island to drive out the French who remained in Santo Domingo. But the French – who finally withdrew from the island in 1809 – brought in reinforcements, forcing Dessalines and Christophe to retreat; a retreat that made gory reading and left a residue of hate on the Dominican side. Dessalines was assassinated in 1806 and Haiti split in two. Christophe ruled as king in the north and center, and Alexandre Petion ruled as president of the west and south.

Christophe published the *Gazette Officielle de L'Etat D'Haiti* in 1808 and, when he proclaimed himself king, changed the name to *Gazette Royale d'Haiti*. It lasted until his death in 1820. Exilien Hertelou, one of Haiti's leading journalists who wrote a history of

Haitian newspapers up to the 1840's, noted that these two newspapers published only official acts, and some foreign newspaper articles. No other newspapers were permitted by either Christophe or Petion. The king wrote letter to American papers and had his decrees published in the New England press.

Petion established *Sentinelle D'Haiti* in 1807, changing its name two years later to *Bulletin Officielle*. *L'Echo*, a literary publication, started in 1813, lasting only three months. A year later, 1813, *Le Telegraphe* – which survived until 1843 – was founded. It also published only official acts and was replaced in 1845 by *Le Moniteur*, the official government gazette, which continues publication today.

All the newspapers under Petion's rule in the west and south were printed on the government press, the only one in the republic. In the north, Christophe had his own royal print shop at Sans Souci. Christophe's secretary, Baron de Vastey, who had been born a slave, was one of the earliest polemicists. His "*Political Remarks…*Concerning Haiti," was published in 1817. An English translation was published in London a year later. The same year, James Baskett published in London his "*History of the Island of St. Domingo: From its First Discovery to the present Period.*"

Petion, preoccupied, as all Haitians at the time, with fears of an invasion from France,

kept out of his neighbors' politics. An exception came in 1816 when he welcomed Simon Bolivar. Defeated by the Spanish the first time, he returned to Haiti where Petion rearmed him for his successful liberation of Venezuela. Petion also provided Bolivar with a printing press, asking only that the press be used to publish a proclamation abolishing slavery in the countries he liberated. Petion asked that his name not be mentioned "in any of your documents." Bolivar sent Petion his ornate gold sword in gratitude to "the author of our liberties." He did not, however, liberate the slaves.

In this newspaper of 1802 not a word about the Haitian revolution.

December 4, 1810 under from page title "Interesting miscellany; Christophe's Proclamation;

Chapter 8

King Henry 1 and Public Relations

An example of how a victor demonizes the vanquished and in so doing creates an image of the country abroad that remains shrouded in darkness.

In *The Salem Gazette* on Tuesday morning April 8, 1821 the offending article appeared on the front page of the New England paper under the title: "Henry Christophe." It was signed by a General Chanlatte, Sen.and dated," Hayitan (sic) 28 Oct.1820. Year of Independence 17."

The Salem Gazette: "The following abominable character of his late sable Majesty we have translated from a paper printed at Cape-Hayitan under the authority of the government, and presented to us by Capt. Larkin Lee on his arrival from that place some time since. Whether it is a faithful picture of the original, we cannot say: whatever vices may have belonged to him, (King Henry Christophe) undoubtedly it was not the policy of those who overthrew him, and succeeded to his power, to conceal. According to this account, he was as cruel as he was absolute, in the exercise of his power."

The long anti- Christophe diatribe was far too personal an attack to be credible as General Chanlatte, (Gen. Juste Chanlatte was Emperor Dessalines's Secretaire-General) describing the King's teeth as "long and sharp after the manner of a cannibal's teeth and the jaw of a shark and heart of a tiger." The General wrote a litany of acts of inhuman brutality which he attributes to Christophe who died by his own hand on the 10th of October, 1820, at ten p.m.in his palace of Sans-Souci.

So Americans, especially New Englanders, who had been given a glowing succession of articles from the Palace of Cape Henry signed by the Henry Christophe himself, were, after his death told he was a "Bloody tyrant". Christophe believed in Public Relation and had kept up correspondences and published articles in North America and England especially after he became King Henry I. in 1811.

In the *New-Hampshire Patriot* on Dec.4, 1810 in a front page article, Christophe's proclamation, appeared. It was addressed to his army after successfully routing the forces of Alexandre Petion from the fortress town of Môle St. Nicolas. We quote:

"Henry Christophe, President and Generalissimo of the land and sea forces of Hayti:
"Soldiers,

"St.Nicholas Môle has succumbed to your arms: the rebellion in this quarter is extinguished, and you have planted in all places the flags of the legitimate authority, rendered so famous already by the numerous triumphs gained over the enemies of liberty.
"A regular siege of twenty days has sufficed to render in ruins the fortresses built by the parricidal hands to the genius of rebellion. In vain a pretended expeditionary army flattered itself to perpetuate intestine division and to pour incense on the altar of error. Your arms in support of the most just of causes have in a few days overturned those edifices, and engulphed in their proud wreck the audacity, the projects and hopes of a new herde of Vendeans."

This long well written proclamation made no mention of Petion and ended with,"
Done at the Palace of Cape Henry,8th October,1810, 7th year of Independence.

Henry Christophe
By the President. The mareschal-de –camp of his Serene Highness. Provost."

Chapter 9

Importance of the Masonic order

by Jack Buta P.M.
Written by: The Freemason Academy

"Wednesday, January 20, 2010:

The country, once known as Hispaniola, began as a French colony in which hundreds of thousands of African slaves worked the sugar plantations under horrific conditions. Many of them were literally worked to death. The news of the French revolution would ignite a bloody revolution and the loss of Haiti led to Napoleon giving up a vast portion of North America in what is known as the Louisiana Purchase.

What is not so widely known, is the important part Haiti played in the liberation of South America, and the spread of the Scottish Rite in France in 1804. The key players in this Masonic history were Estienne Morin, originator of what we know today as the Morin Rite, Alexandre Francois Auguste Comte de Grasse, and Jean Baptiste Delahogue (two of the eleven co-founders of the Scottish Rite), Simon Bolivar, (Freemason and Liberator of Columbia, Panama, Peru, and Bolivia), and a Haitian who would become the first President of a United and Free Haiti, by the name of Jean Pierre Boyer.

Estienne Morin, who had been involved in high degree Masonry in Bordeaux, France since 1744, founded an "Ecossais" lodge (Scots Masters Lodge) in the city of Le Cap Francais, on the north coast of the French colony of Saint-Domingue (Haiti) in 1747. Around 1763 Morin compiled a Masonic Rite consisting of twenty-five degrees known as "The Rite of the Royal Secret," or "Morin's Rite." This Rite became quite popular in the New World and its Degrees would be incorporated into the 33 Degree Scottish Rite in 1801.

Jean Baptiste Delahogue, a French Plantation owner in Haiti, who would become Comte de Grasse's father-in-law, and Haitian born Jean Pierre Boyer were practitioners of the Morin Rite.

De Grasse, arrived in Haiti in 1789 just in time to witness the opening battles of the Haitian revolution. Both he and his family, including Delahogue, were forced to flee the island for Charleston, S. Carolina four years later in 1793. For the next few years he was forced to bide his time while he waited for an opportunity to rejoin the battle.

By 1799 news of the arrival from France of General Hedouville in Haiti reached de Grasse and he volunteered his services and immediately set sail for the island. Upon his arrival in Santo Domingo he was informed that the General had been driven off the island and de Grasse was taken captive and cast into prison shackled hand and foot. Only the intervention of the American Consul prevented his death and he was released on the condition he return directly to Charleston.

The next year the French Schooner, la Vengeance arrived in Norwich from Haiti. An 1856 article written in the Magazine of American History Vol. 13, entitled "An Old Masonic Charter", describes the Masonic regalia and documents found on a young prisoner on board. The following is a short except from that article.

"Among the prisoners sent to Norwich was a mulatto who had been a lieutenant under Rigaud. His name was Jean Pierre Boyer, a native of Port-au-Prince . . . In his possession, at the time of his capture, were found a complete set of the regalia and jewels of a Masonic Lodge and a variety of Masonic documents, such as forms for admission to the Fraternity, catechisms of the various degrees from an Entered Apprentice up to Perfect Master, communications from the Grand Orient at Paris, and a Warrant, or Charter, (for the Morin Rite) signed by none other than Estienne Morin . . . Boyer made his way to France, where he was well received by Napoleon, then First Consul, and from whom he obtained a commission in General LeClerc's expedition, which sailed for St. Domingo in January, 1802."

In February 1802, General Charles Leclerc arrived with tens of warships and 12,000 French troops to bring Saint-Domingue under more control. Gens de couleur Petion, Boyer and Rigaud returned with him in the hope of securing power in the colony.

At the same time, de Grasse was appointed the Grand Inspector General and Grand Commander of the French West Indies for the Scottish Rite with his father-in-law serving as Deputy. Within 30 days de Grasse, now under orders from General LeClerc, sailed for Haiti once more.

For about eight months Boyer and de Grasse fought along side each other but in October, Petion, Boyer, and Rigaud, joined with the nationalist forces. In 1803 the few remaining French were forced to surrender and de Grasse was again facing death. However, someone in the Petion regime spared his life and allowed him free passage to France. The candidates for granting such clemency in Haiti in 1803 are few indeed and the most likely would have been Boyer.

In 1804 Haiti was actually a divided country with two presidents. Six years later however, most of the country was loyal to Petion with Boyer as his aid and heir.

Enter Simon Bolivar, Freemason and freedom fighter.

On July 5, 1810 Civil War broke out in Venezuela; the long awaited fight for freedom was underway. It would eventually cost Bolivar his family's fortune and his life. When the revolt failed, Bolivar was forced to take to the jungle to avoid capture by the royalists. He made his way to London and pleaded for help from the British but had to settle for vague promises. Undaunted he returned home and took command of the revolutionary forces for a year. He held on to Caracas only to be ousted once more by the Royalists. This time he reversed his direction and followed the rivers into Columbia and captured Bogota. By now he was low on men and arms and had to flee to the coast and take refuge in Haiti. By now Boyer was the Vice President under Petion and it was undoubtedly his influence which resulted in Bolivar obtaining the supplies and men he needed on nothing more than a promise to set free any slaves he encountered.

This was the turning point of the campaign. He landed in Venezuela in 1816, and took Angostura (now Ciudad Bolivar). There he was named President of Venezuela. Events continued to unfold in his favor and three years later he marched into Columbia and defeated the Spaniards in the city of Boyar, liberating the territory of Colombia. He then returned to Angostura and led the congress that organized the original republic of Colombia.

At the National Palace the bust of President for Life Jean-Pierre Boyer (1818-43) photo the author

On February 16, 1812, New York Prince Hall Freemasons named both their first Lodge (and later a Grand lodge) after the very popular Jean-Pierre Boyer. In 1818 Petion died and two years later the self-styled King Henry Christopher in the north committed suicide leaving Boyer as the first President of a unified Haiti. One can only wonder what might, or might not, have happened if de Grasse and Bolivar had not run into Boyer when they did."

(Author photo)
Boyer's grave in Pere Lachaise in Paris where he died in 1850. He ruled as president for life from 1818 to 1843.

Chapter 10

First Journalist executed

Gen. Jean-Pierre Boyer, who became president of Haiti upon the death of Petion in 1818, believed, as did his predecessors, that there was a limit to freedom of speech and took drastic action against a foreign journalist he had helped to establish a newspaper in the country.

Felix Darfour, born in Darfour, Senegal, and taken to France as a boy by a French General began to write under the pen name "African Darfour." He arrived in Haiti at the beginning of the Boyer presidency. Madiou, in his history of Haiti, reports that Darfour, "having known that there was a state in America where people of his race were governing themselves, had sailed on a ship from le Havre (France) to Haiti, agreeing to pay for his passage upon his arrival at his destination. Boyer gave him a warm welcome and paid all his expenses, including his passage to Haiti. Darfour soon started a weekly newspaper with a promise from Boyer that it would be printed at state expense, with newsprint furnished from the state stores. In addition, according to Alexis Beaubrun Ardouin (*Etudes sur l'histoire d'Haiti; Paris 1853-1860*), Boyer took a dozen annual subscriptions to the newspaper, paying in advance from his own pocket. Other functionaries and private citizens followed the president's example.

The newspaper, *L'Eclaireur*, began publication on Aug. 5, 1818 and, reports **Madiou**, was "quite coolly received because it was without interest." Ardouin, an ardent Boyerist, concurred, stated, "if there were not more subscribers, it is because Darfour writes in a mediocre manner." The Saint-Louis de Gonzague library in Port-au-Prince has copies of the fourth and fifth issue. The writing is not very attractive and one can, without taking sides, prefer to read *L'Abeille* of Milscent, its opponent. From the beginning, *L'Eclaireur* and *L'Abeille* dedicated much of their space attacking each other.

"One must confess that the Darfour style was often defamatory. `What presumption!...O dear compatriots...Ah the corrupt ones...Haitian what an example of wisdom to be followed..."

However during the *L'Abeille* and *L'Eclaireur* polemic, both sides used pretentious style. *L'Abeille* : "The world was in the dark, *L'Eclaireur* came out and light spread on the Universe... I am afraid coming too close to this prefect sun it could suffer the fate of *d'Icarus*...but *L'Abeille* will not however let its wings be pulled without making the point of its dart felt."

Darfour answered: "The light of *L'Eclaireur* dissipating the darkness that envelops the world has produced an unhappy effect on *L'Abeille*, which could not sustain its very bright light." Darfour filled his paper with unending quotes from Montesquieu and with gossip concerning the love life of a man of color and a white woman. Or the activities of the good-for-nothing young Parisians; but sometimes he used a more virile style when he warned Haitians against some articles that were published in the press in France that were designed to prevent the French government from recognizing Haiti's independence.

However Darfour overstepped the journalistic boundary--especially in Haiti--when he sent to the house of deputies a petition that Beaubrun Ardouin in his *Etudes Sur l"Histoire d'Haiti* (Vol. 9 chapter 4.1853-60) says when it was read, "its content inspired horror and indignation among the members." But Beaubrun Ardouin as a Boyerist may have exaggerated and there appears to have been a nucleus of discontent in parliament as it was read publicly by members of the Chamber. So great was Boyer's anger that the legislators who appeared to have backed the petition were excluded from the chamber--a nice way of saying they were booted out. Ardouin says Darfour faced a military tribunal and was promptly judged even though the offending petition had been lost. He was summarily condemned to death. He could not be shot the following day as it was Sunday, so they shot him on Monday. Madiou notes that Darfour was taken Sept.2, 1818 to the cemetery in Port-au-Prince where the firing squad awaited along with the public. But when the first volley only wounded the journalist, he gathered together his jaw smashed by a bullet and as the firing squad reloaded he managed to address the soldiers through his broken jaw: "My brothers aim well as not to make me suffer." They did and African Darfour died the first newsman executed by the government.

Darfour's execution produced a significant early blot on Haiti's journalistic history. At the same time, the period was to produce a remarkable definition of the ideal journalist, one that remains valid nearly two centuries later. It was provided by Jules Solime Milescent, in the Jan. 1, 1818 issue of his *l'Abeille Haitienne* as reported by Haitian Emanuel Justin Castera's thesis presented at the Universite Libre de Bruxelles and entitled "*Aux Origines de la Press Haitienne – 1764-1850.*" It read:

"The craft of a journalist imposes duties upon him; he must not be merely an echo of news that comes from the four corners of the world, or the faithful copyist of his government's decrees. He is destined to more distinguished functions; like a magistrate who looks after the public's safety, the morality, the execution of the laws, he denounces abuses, propagates useful truths, conciliates the minds, and strives for the general well-being; free defender of the people's rights and zealous servant of the government, he must repulse the venomous attacks of any enemy, the characters of which merit only a sovereign contempt."

Milescent was born in 1778 at Grande Riviere du Nord of an old colonial family. (His father had married Francoise Bernard, a free black, with whom he had eight children. He was beheaded on the guilliotine in France.) Milescent became president of the Chamber of Deputies under Boyer. He died in 1842 during a devastating earthquake in Cap Haitien.

Chapter 11

Espana Bobo to Spanish Haiti

When the French were pushed from the Eastern side of the island it became Spanish once more, an era known as Espana Bobo (Silly Spain). President Boyer accepted the invitation from Dominicans and proclaimed Spanish Haiti on Nov. 30, 1821, which it remained until 1844. Any enthusiasm for Boyer's rule was short lived. He reasserted the principle of "indivisibility" over the island. As Rayford W.Logan (*Haiti and the Dominican Republic,* Oxford University Press, 1968 observed: "This restoration of Haitian sovereignty began a twenty-one year period of 'ethiopianization,' which constitutes the most effective chapter in the Dominican indictment of Haitians."

The Dominicans were treated as second class citizens and humiliated. Many Haitians disapproved of Boyer's actions. He closed the New World's oldest university in Santo Domingo and his army acted as a colonial force of occupation. The rare Dominican praise for President Boyer was his introduction of the Napoleon Code.

During the period of the Haitian occupation, journalism suffered its darkest days and as such became virtually extinct. There were three separate governors in Santo Domingo during Boyer's rule. All followed his totalitarian example, including suppression of free speech. Boyer was finally ousted and fled into exile on March 13, 1843, succeeded by a provisional government headed by Charles Riviere-Herard. A year later, on Feb. 28, 1844, Dominicans successfully, rose up against the Haitian force and proclaimed their independence.

Manuel Amiama, a well known journalist and professor, recounts the evolution of journalism on Dominican side of the island in his 1932 book: *El Periodismo en La Republica Dominicana.* Boyer's ouster, says Amiama, marked the beginning of what he called "The First Republic, "and of journalism in the country.

The first effort at indigenous journalism had actually come in 1821 with *Telegrafo Constitucional*, which offered a much more imaginative than informative depiction of colonial life. It survived only a month and it was not until the First Republic that a serious journalistic effort was seen.

While the first 16 years were not notably prolific, they did produce *El Dominicano*, in 1845, which many considered the first true newspaper in the Dominican Republic. It was a four-page periodical printed on premium quality paper which concerned itself mainly with defending national interests and the principles of the separatist movement. The First Republic saw the rise and fall of a multitude of other newspapers, most of them were idealistic, political and fanatical in nature, and as ephemeral as the political parties of that restless period.

Following the First Republic came a short period (1861-1865) of annexation to Spain, a time when only two publications existed. *El Progreso* concerned itself mostly with philosophical, literary and financial affairs and support for a river navigation project. *La Razon,* on the other hand, supported a river canal project. Although the Spanish greatly restricted Dominican writers' freedom of expression on the island, they did voice their opinions in periodical outside the country.

The Second Republic followed the Spanish annexation period and with it came a great sense of national pride. Amiama divides the Second Republic into five separate periods, the first from 1865 to establishment of the first daily newspaper in 1882. it was also a period characterized by mainly politically ideological periodicals. Some backed and others opposed a constitutional government. *El Provenir*, grew to such acclaim and respect that it was often cited in heated political debates.

The second period of the Second Republic (1882-1899) gave birth to the daily press. Although previous periodicals had great philosophical and political implications, it was not until this period that contemporary public life became a lengthy discussion topic. *El Telegrama*, the first periodical dedicated to daily news events, was founded in 1882. it gained considerable public acceptance, inspiring other periodicals to increase both the frequency of publication and the amount of news that appeared in them. Santo Domingo alone saw the birth of 12 newspapers in this period.

The third phase of the Second Republic begins with the 1899 assassination of President Ulises Heureaux, which gave rise to both greatly increased partisan politics and journalism. The country counted fourteen governments and seven revolutionary movements from 1899 to 1916.

It was a complicated time in which partisanship dominated the columns of the many newspapers that appeared and disappeared.

The fourth period, or The Intervention, says Amiama,, "is without doubt the most glorious moment lived by the national press in Santo Domingo." It is so named because of the U.S. intervention from 1916 to 1924 and which united, a then divided national press against a common foe, the United States. According to Amiama, "it was so united, the national press, to the battle of resistance, that it freed the national spirit against the intervention, against its men, against its methods, against its influences, that to write the history of the national press in that time is to write the history of the intervention itself, with all if its errors and mediocracies."

1n "El President Heureaux y los gobiernos haitianos (1887-1899)", Pastor Vásquez Frías writes about the origin of Ulises Heureaux." On 21 oct 1845 "una mujer de piel oscura" named Josefa Lebert a native of Saint Thomas gave birth to a son whom she named Hilarión. His father D'Assas Heureaux was a resident of Puerto Plata. Heureaux received schooling in a Methodist mission and then joined a revolt against Spain in the early 1860s, distinguishing himself as a soldier. Following Dominican independence and years of internal chaos, Heureaux became president in 1882 after exiling Luperón, his former leader. As the strongman in 1884 and 1886 he selected his country's presidents while he continued to direct the government; from 1887 to his death he ruled officially and uninterruptedly after abolishing the constitutional barrier against reelection. He was assassinated in Moca July 26, 1899.

The first years of the American intervention were marked by large degrees of censorship, but as World War I ended and the international community was inspired by sentiments of peace and justice, the United States began to reconsider its position in the Dominican Republic. Relaxation of censorship in 1921 was among the first effects of Washington's changing attitudes.

The fifth period of the second republic took place between 1924 and 1933 and is mostly characterized by technological advances. Cable communication gave way to more international news, and newer and better printing presses saw the birth of lengthier publications and the rise of Rafael (Chapita) Trujillo.

One of the nicest things that could be said of Boyer was that he was an "obscurantist"--a president who didn't believe in education so the school system on both sides of the island suffered. Whatever was done at the time was mostly personal initiative, such as the *History of Haiti* by Thomas Madiou. He began his enormous work in 1830, and it was published in 1845. There was also a bad trait that had begun and continued. Whatever was started under a president was abandoned, or worse, undone by his successor. As little was begun under Boyer there was little to destroy say his critics.

During Spanish-Haiti, *L'Etoile Haitienne* was published in Santo Domingo in 1821 under the editorship of Caminero. It did not last very long nor did it touch any controversial subjects.

M.A. Amiama, in his 1933 book, *"El Periodismo en la Republica Dominicana,"*notes, *"The Listin Diario*, founded in 1889, long enjoyed the reputation of being one of the most independent newspapers in Latin America. Until its suppression, by Trujillo, with other opposition newspapers, in 1942, it was the most influential newspaper in the republic, and, together with Fabio Fiallo's *La Bandera Libre*, denounced the American occupation."

Chapter 12

SOULOUQUE'S INVASION

Boyer's 27 years in power were followed by four presidents between April 1843 and February 1847. Those who occupied the violent musical chairs (The music was provided by guns) were; Charles Riviere Herard, Philippe Guerrier. Jean-Louis Pierrot and Jean-Baptiste Riche. Each also sought unsuccessfully to hold onto the Dominican Republic. Herard in 1844 faced an uprising by Acaau and his Piquet movement **in** the South.

Then, in March 1847, elderly Faustin Solouque was made president. His rough Zinglins (Makouts) supporters demanded he be made president-for-life instead he declared himself Emperor Faustin 1 two years later.

Soulouque tried unsuccessfully to re-conquer the Spanish side, reportedly motivated by the fear that France was serious about retaking possession of the Dominican again. It was also a time when there was talk of the United States considering an annexation request from the Eastern side of the island. There were other fears as well. Slave traders had for many years been kidnapping Haitians and selling them as slaves in Puerto Rico where slavery existed until 1872, and Cuba, where it lasted until 1898.

Soulouque was twice repulsed by the Santana Brothers – in 1849 and 1850 – in his attempts to retake the Dominican Republic. As he retreated to Haiti, he burned and savaged the countryside in the manner of Dessalines' retreating army. But Soulouque, a tyrant, treated his own people as badly as the Dominicans, and was finally ousted in 1859 and Fabre Geffrard took power.

Paul Dhormoys, in his book "*A Visit to Soulouque's Country,*" describes how he left the French army to enroll in the ....Dominican army being formed by Pedro Santana to resist the invasion by Soulouque, then later left the Dominican army as well. Encouraged by a friend, he had been offered the rank of captain, six thousand francs and a free passage to Santo Domingo. He described it as a lovely country, protected by both France and England, and was told it would be a gallant deed to defend it against that "ferocious Soulouque who sought to devour it."

He, along with some French companions, resigned Santana's army in disgust after spending some time in the Eastern side of the island, noting: "That republic is far from having attained that it was aiming for. After 14 years of existence, it is far less advanced than on the morrow of her birth. All she thinks of is to give away her territory to whom will be willing to buy it. It has no repulsion for Americans with their color prejudice. All Dominicans, black or mulatto, have called themselves so much '*blancs de la tiere*,' that they have come to believe they are really white and come directly from the Spanish without any mixture. They are convinced it is the sun that has blackened their skin and kinked their hair, and that the Americans give them their places, their grades with the fabulous pay reserved for Americans. The American emissaries do nothing to dissuade them, on the contrary! They give the Dominicans all sorts of fabulous promises. What is going to become of this country

FABRE GEFFRARD
PRESIDENT DE LA REPUBLIQUE D'HAITI

dominated by a ferocious and venal dictator (Santana)? That race has inherited only their vanity from the Spanish and, from the mulattos, only their cowardice and their ingratitude."

In 1859, Gen. Fabre Nicolas Geffrard ousted Soulouque whose empire died with him. Geffrard reversed Haiti's policy, and showed empathy toward the Dominicans. When Santana called upon Spain to return and take over the country as a protectorate, Geffrard objected and refused to recognize Spanish rule next door. A Spanish fleet visited Port-au-Prince, rattling its canons in a menacing manner but the diplomatic Geffrard was able to calm down the Spanish admiral. Some years later, under Haitian president Pierre Theoma Boisrond- Canal, the Spanish "comandante" Autran , appeared off Port-au-Prince, with a fleet for the same reasons and, again, the Haitian president employed charm and the two adversaries parted friends with an "abrazo."

Meanwhile, in the Dominican Republic, Fernando Arturo de Merino became provisional president on Sept. 11, 1880, presiding for two years over what is considered a period of enlightenment. He began publication of the *Boletin Judicial.*

The Haitian press of the entire period is filled with examples of atrocities committed by the Spanish and the agents of Santana against Dominican patriots. Some Haitians crossed the border and fought alongside their Dominican neighbors in a guerrilla action against Spanish troops. For years, a considerable two-way trade existed between the two countries. It was a tradition, as well, for revolutionaries of both countries to seek refuge across the border. That halted with the American occupation of the Dominican Republic and the rise to power Rafael Trujillo.

In order to understand the functioning of the Haitian press, it is very important to observe that a great number of papers appear during revolution or the overthrow of a president, and disappear after the commotion, when they have served their purpose, or suppressed by the victors. It happened in 1946, and happened in 1930. It also happened in 1959.

On March, 8, 1876 Geffrard, in an effort to calm public unrest, declared freedom of the press. It was too late. Ten days later he was off aboard ship taking the familiar route to exile in Jamaica.

As often happens, after the long reign of Boyer there was a scramble to fill the presidency. Nissage Saget's Presidency was interrupted after a month by populist Sylvain Salnave who took power in May 1867.

Salnave had been violently opposed by the bourgeoisie and even more violently supported by his partisans: the black middle class and the proletariat. A fine intellectual, Demesvar Delorme, sided with him. After many bloody battles, Salnave was bombed out of the palace and shot on the smoldering ruins. For two months his partisans were searched for and summarily shot. With Salnave dead, Saget took back his presidency and ruled until 1874. During those intense 5 years of murderous politics, 15 newspapers were born: 10 at Port-au-Prince, 1 at Cap-Haitien, 1 at Saint Marc, 2 at Jacmel, 1 at Aux Cayes. It was a considerable number when one stops to think that it is only in the sixties that Geffrard started his reform of the schools and signed a covenant (Concordat) with the Vatican to receive a competent French clergy for parochial schools. In 1860 there were 10,000 students in 54 schools for the whole of Haiti.

(Photos courtesy CIDIHCA).

Salomon and his French wife.

Chapter 13

National and Liberal Parties.

From its beginning, it was a partisan press that evolved in Haiti. The journalists were not reporters, but polemicists and proselytizers, preaching their cause in their work and, at the same time, attacking their adversaries. As a result, they were frequently jailed, exiled or challenged to a duel. In fact, Port-au-Prince had a thriving "Salle d'Armes," a business where one learned to use a sword in order to be able to use a pen. Such a partisan and often subsidized press considered advertising a burden imposed by economic imperative and not as a condition of its existence or even its independence. In 1888, the newspaper *L'Union* carried this notice: "We lack space for our advertisements; they will appear in the next edition"

Despite all the difficulties of the early years, Haiti did give rise to some fearless journalists, often engaging in ideological battles to defend their beliefs. In the time of the National and Liberal parties with Jean-Pierre Boyer Bazelais and Edmond Paul leading the Liberals with their slogan, *"power to the most capable"*. The Nationals led by a famous writer and orator, Demesvar Delorme, had a more democratic slogan, *"power to the most numerous."* Both parties were basically in agreement on good government but separated by the evil demon; color! Boyer-Bazelais had met Edmond Paul at the *Civilsateur* having served a decade in public administration. The friendship of the two intellectuals was to last a political lifetime.

To the detriment of intellectuals, no matter their slogans the truth was that power had been the domain of the military and Generals had chased each other in and out of power since the beginning of the Haitian state. However, there were efforts to break the cycle of military leaders, the men with guns.

Following a yellow fever epidemic, a vocal fight in parliament moved to the streets. For three days Liberal party members including Hannibal Price and Edmond Paul, all well known writers, under the leadership of Jean-Pierre Boyer Bazelais, grandson of President Boyer, led their forces against the regime of President General Boisrond Canal. The government's artillery finally destroyed Bazelais' home, which was serving as Liberal headquarters. The home of Edmond Paul was also destroyed. Fire destroyed the city center, and among the 150 killed were Bazelais's two brothers. On July 17, General Boisrond Canal fled with his family to Saint Thomas, Virgin Islands. A month later Bazelais continued the fight in Gonaives, lost and fled to exile in Jamaica. On August 19, 1879, Lysius Félicité Salomon who had returned from 17 years in exile in France on 12 May 1876 to become the darling of the National party. was chosen President by the "Assemblee nationale" taking power on 26 October 1879.

The fight between the 'nationals" and the "liberals" had not ended with the triumph of the Nationals led by Lysius Salomon. For the liberals who lost, Salomon's decade in power was yesterday, such were the emotion born of his rule. "This meat is tough as Salomon's hide." complained an elderly member of a liberal family, even 75 years later.

 Able and learned men were in both camps and the fight raged both in the Congress and in the press. It was also physical and bloody. 23 newspapers were born: 18 at Port-au-Prince, 2 at Cap-Haitien, 2 at Gonaives, 1 at Jacmel.

When Salomon was overthrown, the fight for succession was between Francois Denys Legitime from the South and Seide Telemaque from the north. Telemaque was killed in a battle in front of the presidential palace, the North refused to accept Legitime. The country was again cut in two just as it was in the time of Petion and Christophe. The fight raged until Legitime went into exile to be succeeded by Florvil Hyppolite from the north. Thirty newspapers were founded in that one year: 20 at Port-au-Prince, 1 at Saint Marc, 3 at Jeremie (hometown of Legitime), 3 at Cap-Haitien, 2 at Jacmel, 1 at Gonaives.

National party leader ,President Salomon.

President Lysius Salomon (President 1879-88) with members of the National party)

Boyer Bazelais (1833 - 1883)
hef de file dé Parti liberal et un des modeles d'Antenor Firmin

A descendant discovers the grave in the Miragoane cemetery where Jean-Pierre Boyer Bazelais is buried.

Brief family biography

Old myths,old gods,old heroes have never died.They are only sleeping at the bottom of our mind, waiting for our call. we have need for them they represent the wisdom of our race. **Stanley Kunitz**

On July 28, 1805, Louis Laurent Bazelais, chief of staff of gen Jean Jacques Dessalines and a signer of the act of independence was promoted to general in command of the Haitian Army. His son Charles Bazelais married Azéma Boyer, daughter of President Boyer.

The discovery of a marriage certificate finally solved an old family doubt. Was Azema the daughter of Joute Lachenais, the famous courtesan who had been the mistress of Haiti first President, Alexandre Petion and then of President Jean-Pierre Boyer and who went into exile with him in France in 1843 after he had ruled for 24 years. The marriage certificate states that Charles Bazelais married Jeanne Francoise Victoire Azema, daughter of President Boyer and Suzanne Miss Sanite. It appears that Suzanne Miss Sanite was Boyer's lady before he took up with the powerful Joute. Among the witnesses at the marriage was Joseph Balthazar Inginac, secretary general of his Excellency President Boyer. Inginac had also been Dessalines' eyes and trusted secretary.

Jean-Pierre Boyer Bazelais, the son of Charles and Azema, was born in Port-au-Prince in 1833. They sent him to France, at age 16 to study at lycée Charlemagne. At 19, he received his licencé in law at the University of Paris. He returned home at age 25 and entered public service. In August 1865, he married Adléda Liautaud of Croix des Bouquets and they had 6 children.

His fight with Salomon forced the family to take exile. The French resident minister, Brudel, made a personal appeal to Salomon to permit the Bazelais family that had fled into the French legation when their home had been destroyed during the fighting. The family included the aged mother of Jean-Pierre Boyer Bazelais, Azema known to her family as Mimi, his young 14 year old son Alexandre, and mostly female family members. Salomon finally agreed they could depart for exile but denied them transport from the French Legation to the dock. Even though the French minister offered his own carriage to the 88-year old family matriarch, Salomon said no to his request. The minister walked with the group holding the French bicolor over them ignoring the hooting and shouting of the angry Salomonists lining the streets from Bois Verna to the waterfront wanting their heads.

In Jamaica where the women worked sewing to support themselves, Alexandre, although a youth, managed to find work with the French builder of the Panama Canal operated by Ferdinand de Lesseps constructor of the Suez Canal. In spite of all their efforts, the French failed.

Chapter 14

Partisan Press

State is the name of the coldest of all cold monsters...The state tells lies in all the tongues of good and evil; and whatever it says is lies—and whatever it has it has stolen. Everything about it is false...All too many are born: for the superfluous the state has invented"

Nietzsche

On May 3, 1883, after 3 years in exile, the Liberal leadership led by Boyer Bazelais landed from Jamaica with 92 men. Their beachhead was Miragoane, a town on the coast, south of Port-au-Prince. They declared their "Revolution" and the liberal and national parties were at war again with Salomon's force bottling up the liberals not only in Miragoane but also in the port towns of Jacmel and Jérémie.

When Salomon's minister of war, Henry Piquant, was killed at Miragoane on September 22, 1883 the anger of Salomon was awesome as Port-au-Prince was *mise a feu et a sang.* It became black against mulatto, the color of a man's skin was his party affiliation and Salomon struck back viciously and indiscriminately in Port-au-Prince. Homes, shops and businesses belonging to *milats* were destroyed in Port-au-Prince and many were killed (1) in what was described as the "Week of blood". The killing prompted European Nations to warn Salomon they would intervene if the killing and looting did not stop. Immediately the killing stopped.

1. There was no reliable casualty figure but sufficient killings to alarm the world. Old family stories are still told of Gen. Salomon on horse- back directing the destroying of mulatto businesses. When a strongly built brick business resisted fire and force, Salomon is said to have ordered a cannon be brought up to do the job.

Boyer Bazelais died of dysentery on 27 of Oct 1883, while the fight continued for another two month. It was the end of the Miragôane affair as well as uprisings in Jacmel and Jérémie. What role did the U.S. play? It added 2 ships to Salomon's navy with which he bombarded Jacmel and Jeremie, and later, aboard the warship Dessalines he inspected the towns he had brought to heel.

In August 1988 having changed the constitution to be reelected Salomon, a tired and sick old man threw in the sponge and return to France, with his French wife. He died six weeks later to be buried in the cimetiere de Passy., not in the same Paris cemetery in which President-for-life Jean Pierre Boyer is buried.

A painting of Jean-Pierre Boyer Bazelais in Miragoane.

In *Jean-Pierre Boyer Bazelais and the drama of Miragoane r*," Dr. Price-Mars wrote while he served as ambassador to the Dominican Republic. He published documents discovered in Miragoane long after the siege had ended. Dr. Price-Mars, not a liberal, concluded after examining these documents that they showed **"traits of character, so noble that they deserve to be noted as pearls of which a community must be proud. Honesty, pride, un-selfishesness, faithfulness, making the supreme sacrifice of life; all briefly stated with simple and candid words."**

BIBLIOTHÈQUE HAITIENNE

Dr. PRICE-MARS

JEAN-PIERRE BOYER BAZELAIS

ET

LE DRAME DE MIRAGOANE

(A PROPOS D'UN LOT D'AUTOGRAPHES)
1883-1884

IMPRIMERIE DE L'ÉTAT
RUE HAMMERTON KILLICK
PORT-AU-PRINCE, HAITI
1948

51

In all those four periods the papers, by their very names, show that they were seeking a fight: *Le Clairon* (The bugle) *La Sentinelle*, *Le Reveil* (The awakening) *Le Ralliement*, *Le Revolutionnaire*, *La Foudre* (The thunder) *L'Appel*, *La Reaction*, *Le Signal…Le Civilisateur*, principal organ of the liberals, founded in 1870, disappears in 1875 when the liberal leadership was forced into exile; whereas *Le Peuple* of J.J. Audain kept up the propaganda of the Nationals until the death of its founder; but *l'Oeil*, launched in 1880 as President Lysius Salomon's propaganda arm, disappeared when he was ousted in 1888. Louis-Joseph Janvier of the National Party had outlined his nationalist ideas in *la Republique d'Haiti et ses Visiteur (1840-83).*

LOUIS-JOSEPH JANVIER
1855-1911

The remarkable, Dr.Louis-Joseph Janvier, wrote, *la Republique d'Haiti et ses Visiteurs* published in Paris in 1883 to be followed by *l'Egalite des Races* and three years later *les Constitutions d'Haiti.*

---000--

Gen. Pierre Theoma Boisrond Canal returned and chased, old and sick, Salomon off to France in 1888. However, General Seide Telemaque marched from Cap Haitien to take power only to learn the provisional government had been handed it to Francois Denys Legitime. Telemaque fought and died in the streets of Port-au-Prince.

The Bazelais family eventually returned to Haiti, and Alexandre Bazelais became a captain in the palace guard, and Aide-de-camp to President Gen Florvil Hyppolite (1889-1896). My mother-in-law, Maria (Mamiche) Bazelais Dreyfuss, the daughter of Alexandre Bazelais, told me a period vodou story. One day we were sitting on the verandah of their modest home at Frères, and I began questioning her about vodou. She began in a defensive manner as so many Haitian do, saying people of her class didn't know much about it and certainly didn't practice it. As the conversation progressed the hold vodou has on people became apparent. "My father, one day, was ordered executed," Mamiche said, explaining that a woman known only as Simbi, with vodou powers entered the palace and waving a veil before the guards disappeared from their sight.. She had been caught at the last moment. before the president's door by an officer whom she had no time to blind. President Hyppolite's mistress was a well known manbo and he believed he had come close to becoming Simbi's victim. He ordered the guards on duty that day all to be executed. Captain

Bazelais was saved from the firing squad only by the general's wife pleading, "Oh not Captain Bazelais." "You see my father used to escort the president's daughters to dances and they were very fond of him." He lost his job but not his life.

Maria (Marmiche) Bazelais Dreyfuss with her youngest daughter, Ginette.

One day on an assignment in Gonaïves I took a photograph of a little child sleeping among the weeds under a little bust of Admiral Killick. Rather than strike his colors and surrender to a German warship, he had blown himself up with his ship wrapped in the Haitian flag. When I told Mamivhe, she replied with the news that Admiral Hamerton Killick had been her god-father and a true hero.

When the newly appointed president, Dumarsais Estime, made the traditional tour of the city in 1946, Mamiche called her employees out of her Bazar du Champs.de Mars, grocery store, across the street from Sylvio Cator's Savoy restaurant, to cheer him. Estime had been a good neighbor and customer, and she made sure they catered to his delicate stomach. Her father, Captain Bazelais went into managing the family plantation at Cabaret called Prince, and died in 1919 at 53 years of age.

Mamiche's husband, engineer Georges Dreyfuss, had a habit of paying a visit to his uncle, historian Edmond Mangones for the New Year. They would discuss his historical research. One New Year, Uncle Edmond told him he had uncovered a document attesting to the fact that General Laurent Bazelais, had given Mallet, a "bon blan" who had signed the act of independence, asylum in his home and then killed him. Gen Bazelais was carrying out Dessalines's orders to kill all the French people in Jeremie and ended the life of his friend. Engineer Dreyfuss told his wife, of "such treachery," her ancestor had killed his.

Georges Corvington made an investigation later to discover that while Mallet appeared white in fact he was a *milat* and---scion of the Mangones family, and questioned Uncle Edmond's report.

Chapter 15

Firmin statesman to warrior

Following nine months of strife, General Florvil Hyppolite, president in the north, became president of the entire republic in October 1889. Anténor Firmin, an outstanding intellectual also from the north, became minister of finance and foreign relations. The building of bridges and the capitals ironmarket (1891) were the hallmark of Hyppolite's six-year term but his execution without trial of suspected plotters made him a tyrant. When president Florvil Hyppolite led his troops to Jacmel after an attack by Merisier Janis and his Piquets and Rasoirs on 24 May, 1896, he suffered a massive heart attack and died on the spot. His death brought forth a popular song *panama'm tombe* as the President's Panama hat had first fallen off his horse.

Another battle raged in 1902 around the talented Antenor Firmin. He was the most formidable intellectual of his time, and one of the most prestigious in the history of Haiti . His *De l'egalite des race humaines* (1885) was an early anthropological work of 650 pages. He had proven himself an extremely able administrator as Minister of Finance and defacto prime minister of President Florvil Hippolyte (1889-1896); and it is largely thanks to his diplomacy that Admiral Bancroft Gherardi backed by the big guns of the U.S. Navy had been kept talking and waiting for the decision on granting the U.S the bay of Môle Saint Nicolas as a coaling station. Finally the negative answer shocked the admiral with the big guns and Haiti stood high. But even the idea of handing over sacred land of the nation caused so much adverse critics. Firmin quit.

Firmin, according to Pradel Pompilus in his 1961, *Histoire de la litterature haitienne* had a profound lifetime attachment to Boyer Bazelais. Both men were determined and tenacious fighters for what they believed were best for the nation.

Even today Firmin is beloved by the youth, admired and trusted by all of those who want a truly modern Haiti. He was detested by all of those who wanted to preserve the status quo and especially by the military, even though a few leaders sided with him such as General Jean Jumeau and Admiral Hamerton Killick. Again the fight was bloody and the intellectual output intense.

Firmin and family.

allied to Firmin, shelled the bay of le Cap. But Firmin's forces failed to dislodge Nord Alexis who destroyed Firmin's home. In September, Killick attacked the German merchant ship carrying arms for the provisional government. In retaliation Germany sent the battleship Panther to order Killick to surrender off Gonaives. The Haitian admiral 's dramatic answer was to order his crew ashore, wrap himself in the flag and blow up himself and his ship, the Crête a Pierrot, into history as yet another heroic deed.

Following Killick's death, Firmin left for exile in Saint Thomas and Nord Alexis became president. However, it was not the end of the fight. On Jan 15, 1908 General Jean Jumeau returned from St.Thomas and Firmin followed and mustered their forces.

In June 1902 admiral Killick

General Nord Alexis

The rebel's shipment of arms was seized by the United States, nevertheless, badly armed, they fought. Jumeau was killed in a battle at the town of Dessalines and victorious Nord Alexis had suspected Firminists executed without trial and they included Massillon Coicou. In 1910 Antenor Firmin died in exile in St Thomas.

MASSILLON COICOU
1867-1908

General Canal

In less than a year, 34 newspapers appear: 20 at Port-au-Prince, 6 at Cap-Haitien, 5 at Aux Cayes, 2 at Gonaives, 1 at Port de Paix.

Chapter 14

The rise of Jean Price-Mars

One of the great pleasures in my early life in Haiti was to accompany Dr.Jean Price Mars and his wife on an afternoon stroll in Petionville. Without doubt, he was a noble man, my hero. His writings helped understand the country.

Between 1881-1883, a smallpox epidemic had ravaged Haiti and the historic town, Grande Riviere du Nord, did not escape the killer. Young Jean Price-Mars managed to survive the disease but his mother did not. It was then that his grandmother took him under her care and he grew into one of the great men of 20th century Haiti.

Thanks to Henoc Dorsinville who had launched *L'Essor* in 1912, the magazine drew Price-Mars to publish Les Corbeaux, a story he had written in Paris while studying medicine. The following year his; *l'Education des Enfants Retardes* appeared in *L'Essor*.

Reform of the education system proved to be his major concern and « Rapport de Jean Price-Mars » appearing in the *Bulletin Officiel du Département de L'Instruction Publique*. In July,1912 his ideas for *"La Reforme de L'Enseignement Primaire"* appeared in *Haïti Littéraire et Scientifique*. In a lecture at the time, he is quoted as warning; "We are living in rancid ideas from the appalling stupidity of an ill-arranged education, and as a result our childish vanity is only satisfied when we repeat like asses the words written for others to glorify "The Gauls our ancestors".

In 1917 at 41 years of age, Price-Mars, set out with his titanic effort to revamp Haiti's national soul with constructive values….reminding the elite of their responsibilities. In the troublesome years ahead he attempted to awaken their conscience by examining the causes of the harmful gap between the élite and the masses. He stressed that division, that constituted two nations, each with its own interest, tendencies and outlook. In his lecture *Economic Domination of Elite,* he called on the upper crust of society to create work of social action and rehabilitation. Rather than heed Price-Mars' warning and advice the élite, after his talk, *The Vocation of the Elite* turned on him in anger. But it was, for him, too important to be side-tracked by their anger and he persevered. While he advocated "black consciousness" he accepted all people no matter their race or color.

Thanks to the influential Dantes Bellegarde, a tall mulatto intellectual, Price-Mars was given a teaching position at Lycée Petion, where he sought the heart and minds of the student in his crusade for acceptance of true Haitian and black values. In 1919, his book on " *La Vocation de l'Elite*" was published. With Pauleus Sannon in 1922, he founded the *Society of Haitian History and Geography.*

It was in 1928 that his master- piece, "*Ainsi Parla L'Oncle*" was published in Paris by imp. De Compiegne. It was his effort to reveal how things were and what truly matters. It sparked the usual anger among the unmovable élite; however no book had such an impact on Haitian thought and literature. It was the seed of an important illuminating work that would be harvested for decades. Writing in the first anniversary of *La Relève* in July 1933, then a senator, Price -Mars complained:

"In a country where the finest things have the worst fate, where more than 50,000 people pretend to be devoted to work of the mind, where the budget of public instruction exceeds several million gourdes annually, how can we explain… that not one publishing house is able to survive on professional activities alone, not one newspaper, not one magazine is able to cover expenses and existence? This is such an anomaly that one could lose his mind in attempting to explain it."

Chapter 15

Black Pride and Black consciousness

In *Ainsi Parla L'Oncle,* Price -Mars, remarked that from the beginning, he believed his country had taken the wrong road to achieve what she thought was her superior destiny: to fashion her thoughts and sentiment after those of former mother country, to look like to identify herself with France. As a result of this long and patient endeavor the Haitians have fallen into a "collective bovarism", that is, seeing themselves other than they really are. But as a result also of an "implacable logic" as the Haitian strove to pretend to be French and wished to establish themselves as such among the people of the world, they were undoing themselves as Haitians –people born in a certain historical framework who have amassed in their souls, as does any other human group, a psychological complex which gives the Haitian community its specific physiognomy. As a consequence, all that is truly indigenous became suspicious and of bad taste in the eyes of the country's élites in their nostalgia for the lost "fatherland." Thus the word "African" has always been and is still the most humiliating adjective that could be applied to the Haitian…'(1)

Dr. Price Mars asks;

"Does Haitian society have a background of oral traditions, legends, tales, songs, riddles, customs, observances, ceremonies an beliefs which are characteristic of it or that it has assimilated so as to give them its personal imprint? And if this folklore exists what is its value from the literary and scientific point of view." Dr. Price -Mars answered stating that no other country has such a rich stock of stories and legends than Haiti.

(2) *(1,2)Jean-Price Mars and Haiti* by Jacques C. Antoine.

His third important book was, "*A Stage of Haitian Evolution*". Price-Mars was a believer and shared in the vision of President Cincinnatus Leconte, the great-grandson of Jean-Jacques Dessalines who was also from his hometown. Sadly that vision died with Cincinnatus Leconte when he was killed in the palace explosion.

Chapter 16

Foreign correspondent's War
"The yellow kids"

The foreign correspondent who reports on, or from, Haiti were often bedeviled by intentional or otherwise misunderstandings of the past, resulting in distorted and tendentious histories. These misunderstandings, or myths, are sometimes perpetuated through schools and universities, or popularized by the media, enforcing the views of ethnic and xenophobic ideologues.

Journalists, although not historians, often are credited with providing the first draft of history. and a rough one it often was. The craft deals in fleeting events that churn and change by the minute, more a snapshot than the composed portraits that true historians paint. In that sense, the journalists can assist historians in their quest for truth and combating the mythmakers. Responsible journalists thus try to set, or keep, the record straight by reporting verified facts as they appear, and refusing to be caught up in the passions of those who try to use the past to rewrite history.

In the United States, the late 19th century became the heyday of "the yellow kids," so named after the color that denoted sensational journalism. Hispaniola was largely spared the attention of these already famous American correspondents, mostly representing New York publications where the editors and publishers pushed the truth to the limit in their battle for readers. These flamboyant and audacious reporters made their name during the Spanish-American War. Havana was across the straits from Key West, Florida and Santiago de Cuba was closer to Haiti, making it possible to evade the Spanish censors in cabling war news.

One of the more famous anecdotes of the war is attributed to William Randolph Hearst, owner of the *New York Journal*, who was in his own war with Joseph Pulitzer's *New York World*. Hearst dispatched Richard Harding Davis and the artist Frederic Remington to Cuba in the winter of 1896-97 to report on the rebellion against the Spanish colonial government. Remington apparently found himself in Havana with little action. He cabled

Hearst: "Everything is quiet. I wish to return." Hearst immediately responded: "Please remain. You furnish the pictures, and I'll furnish the war."

More than 100 foreign correspondents were to cover the Spanish-America War, in large part because it was so accessible. Filing stories to their home offices was among the difficulties, with Key West, Florida, only 90 miles away, becoming the filing point of choice. The author Stephen Crane, among those assigned to cover the war, noted that news that arrived in Key West as a mouse was invariably cabled north as an elephant.

Sharply attired even in war, their war.

Stephen Crane ,author of *Red Badge of Courage* as news correspondent along with Frederic Remington as he was sketched by Artist C E. Akers of *The London Times* in 1898 .

Many of the newsmen found themselves off the coast of eastern Cuba and the city of Santiago de Cuba, where their newspapers had chartered boats – often leaving the journalists themselves to pay for coal and provisions because money did not arrive from their newspaper's home offices. At times, they were fired on by U.S. warships, believing them to be Spanish, and chased by Spanish vessels, believing them to be spies. Rushing to file in Port Antonio, Jamaica, one group of correspondents decided it would be faster to cross the Windward Passage and file from Môle St. Nicolas, Haiti.

Joyce Milton recounted the incident in her 1990 book, "*The Yellow Kids*," observing that: "The presence of warships in the Caribbean had unsettled Haiti's precarious political equilibrium, and the correspondents arrived in le Môle St. Nicolas just as the army was in the last stages of putting down a coup attempt. The governor's palace was cordoned off, the cable office was closed, and the local merchants were unwilling to load coal on an American ship. Fortunately, when the governor, be- medaled with gold-epaulette made his appearance, Stephen Crane got him talking and discovered that the official had formerly been a butler for a family in New Rochelle, New York. Suddenly Crane and the butler were the best of friends, and the visit ended with the correspondents throwing a party on the beach for the entire provincial army, with rum at forty cents per gallon dispensed via a hose." At the end,

Crane decided not to file his story, complaining that he did not see the sense of so many competing writers scrambling to cable home news stories that were essentially the same.

There was one that was not. On June 4, 1898, filing from Port-au-Prince to New York, an Associated Press correspondent scooped the other newsmen, by breaking the story of a U.S sailor's heroic sinking of a collier at the entrance of Santiago harbor bottling up the Spanish fleet inside.

Chapter 17

U.S. Occupation of Hispaniola

The United States dispatched the Marines to Haiti in 1915 and to the Dominican Republic a year later. The Dominican occupation ended in 1924 while Haiti's lasted another 10 years. The "Yellow kids" who had survived were already too busy working on their memoirs to cover these interventions and there was little firsthand coverage of the landings and the early years of the occupation. World War I had become the big story.

Freedom of the press was limited by the American occupation force and it kept the national penitentiary cells occupied by journalists and writers to the point one cell became known as *Le Jolibois* named after a crusading and fearless newsman called Joseph Jolibois Jr. editor of *Courier Haitien*. Jolibois and Georges Petit received accolades from Price-Mars for their progressive writing.

Haitian presidents, Philippe Sudre Dartiguenave (Aug.12, 1915-22), Louis Borno (May, 1922-30), and then Sténio Vincent (1930-41) served under the Occupation forces. During that period several outstanding writers broke ranks with the élite. The emotions and ideas that possessed these writers appeared in print. They were conscious of the shocking in-balance in a society that was cast in stone, with all its behavioral and social deficiencies---living side by side with the poor majority as if they existed on separate planets. Haitian nationalist newsmen and writers took up their pens and wrote in whatever magazine or newspaper remained open. Their vision of reality clashed with that of the governments and occupation authority. It was a time of awakening of consciousness. As Camus wrote in *Rebel*, "it is not one who believes in nothing, but one who does not believe in what exists."

Elie Guerin became a well known journalist who gave up farming to strike nationalist blows against the U.S. occupation in his weekly, *Haiti Integral*. Guerin joined the two other patriots Joseph Jolibois jr of *Courier Haitien* and George J. Petit of *le Petit Impartial,* as regular cellmates in the National Penitentiary for their anti- occupation commentary. It was no joke. Under Martial Law the authorities handed down stiff hard labor jail sentences.

Prisoners were issued identical striped prison garb called *rad makak* and they had to work even to breaking up stones.

In 1938 Carl Brouard of *la Revue Indigene* launched *les Griots* moving a step further from *indigenisme*. Lorimer Denis and Dr. François Duvalier gave their views. The mover of the group was Louis Diaquoi, a talented writer who also wrote for the newspaper *National Action*. He died in 1932 at age 23.

Between 1804, when independence was declared and 1950, Haiti had 885 newspapers, according to M. Bissainthe in the "*Dictionnaire de Bibliographie Haitienne*," published by Scarecrow Press in 1951. Only *Le Nouvelliste*, founded in 1898, and *Le Matin*, founded in 1907, continued to publish, both of which Haitians sometimes refer to as "musique Palais," referring to music by the Palace Band which plays "Hail to the Chief" for every president. But they were survivors, especially *Le Nouvelliste*. The capable Clement Magloire of *Le Matin* unfortunately was followed by descendants ignorant of the rudimental ethics of journalism. The family exception was Clement Magloire fils –who was better known as Magloire St.Aude, the realist poet, whose work appeared in *Les Griot* in 1938.

After the concordat was signed in 1860 the Roman Catholic Church became the official state religion. Communication was mostly though Church bulletins, pamphlets and pastoral letters. In 1896, Monsignor Francois-Marie Kersuzan in Cap Haitien launched the newspaper *La Croix* with its editorial goal, the eradication of vodou. *La Croix* gathered recognition with its leading the crusade again vodou. In 1897 having been moved to the capital *La Croix* became a victim of the church's crusade and was prudently closed. In 1912 the Church published *le Bulletin de Notre Dame* but it was not until 1930 it found its voice with a brand new daily newspaper *La Phalange*. Francois Duvalier was to close all opposition newspapers, magazines, and eventually, *La Phalange, L'Eglise en Marche* and *Rond Point*.

Chapter 18

Heroic Rebels

The light still shines on rebels of that era especially the well known writer Jacques Roumain. In the shadows is the lesser known fighter, Max Hudicourt. Both were born in 1907 and came from similar background, the ranks of the privileged. Jacques Roumain was from a family of wealthy land owners who, like his brothers, studied agronomy in Europe. A radicalized Jacques Roumain returned from Europe in 1927 and became a militant nationalist resulting in his being imprisoned twice in 1928, accused of seditious activity. Prison was no joy, even in those days, and Roumain contracted malaria in a cell in the national penitentiary. While much has been written about Jacques Roumain little has appeared about his friend Max Hudicourt.

In 1931 Roumain published the novel *la Montagne Ensorcelee* (The bewitched Mountain) and Dr. Price-Mars in the preface wrote, "The young novelist has evoked in beautiful pages the picturesque and dramatic life of our peasants... of this life he has marvelously brought forth what makes both its charm and horror: faith."

Max Hudicourt, a skilled orator, also wrote poetry of a classical kind and preferred not to be published. He devoted his efforts as a civil rights lawyer, to the more practical deeds such as fighting for the worker and the under-privileged majority. The son of Lelio Hudicourt, a much respected general practitioner and professor at the faculty of medicine, and, Henriette Rouzier, from an old Methodist family, her mother being a Clerie of Jeremie.

The Hudicourt family were in the 18th century residents of Riviere Froide, south of Port-au-Prince. Upon graduation from medical school, Lelio Hudicourt, was assigned to Jeremie as the medical doctor. Jeremie became his home after meeting his wife, Henriette Rouzier. They raised seven children .It was a family driven by education and they added pillars to the Methodist community of Jeremie. Eventually Lelio returned to Port-au-Prince to teach at the medical faculty.

His brother Pierre (he had changed his birth name from Wilberforce-- after the British abolitionist---to Pierre) had his first taste of politics as a youth traveling as secretary to Edgar Numa from Cayes to Port-au-Prince on orders of François Denis Légitime who became

President in December 1888 for a 7 year term and lasted only 9 months as he was overthrown by Gen Florvil Hyppolite. In the years that followed Pierre became a well known lawyer and senator, and married Therese Rossignol of Desdunes. They had no children..

Max was the eldest son in Lelio's family that included two other sons Pierre, who became a diplomat and whose son Jean-Pierre fought and died with Hector Riobe, fighting against the Duvalier dictatorship. Georges (Dos) was a longtime university professor and leading ophtalmologist while his doctor wife, Edith Dreyfuss was also a professor at the medical faculty. They had eleven children. Of Max's four sisters, three were teachers. One was married to deputy Rossini Pierre Louis of Bainet, who became a victim of Francois Duvalier.

The Hudicourt family home was in Ruelle Piquant next door to the Lalue corner residence of Dantes Bellgarde in Port-au-Prince. Uncle Pierre and wife Therese had a summer house in Petionville where Lelio's family were often guests. While not poor, his parents were of moderate means with a sizeable family.

After primary studies Max Hudicourt, attended college in Port-au-Prince, first at Saint Martial, then at the Lycee National where instruction was provided by Haitians of considerable culture like Pauleus Sannon and Price-Mars. He went on to study law, and to pay his way took up the management of a coffee preparation establishment at Leogane for the Vital family. On graduation, he worked at the Contributions (Tax office) to help with his law practice.

Max's radical side was soon apparent, and, like other intellectuals of the twenties, he believed that Marxism could possibly be applicable to Haiti. However, much of his time was dedicated to defending his less fortunate compatriots, mostly workers involved in labor accidents and labor conflicts. He was listed as a dangerous radical by big business, the government, and U.S. occupiers. Max married, a daughter of their neighbor, Dantes Bellegarde, an important intellectual who had founded the paper *La Ronde* in 1898, which is perhaps why Max called his paper, *La Nouvelle Ronde* founded in 1925. It was Max who had Antonio Vieux, a black , and Philippe Thoby-Marcelin, a mulatto, both 21, write together their thoughts on Haitian literature; "For a Haitian literature to have existed it would have been necessary for the works to reflect more of the aspirations, the temperament ,the very soul of our country…Our elders have produced some works of worth. However, they have not produced works that were profoundly ours. The Haitian soul must be uncovered and analyzed in its bareness. Only by doing that can we get the originality that has been sought after so far away, except where it was possible to find it." Others who wrote in *La Nouvelle*

Ronde that had a very brief existence in 1927, as did the magazine *la Trouée,* included Camille Large ("La littérature haitienne de 1896 »), Philippe Thoby-Marcelin (La littérature d'hier et celle de demain)and Andre Liautaud, (Cendre et flammes d'Edmond Laforest).

The next publication was, *la Revue Indigene.* with the same group of editors, Roumain, Hudicourt and Normil Sylvain among other writers. The impressive list of *la Revue Indigene* collaborators grew to include Emile Roumer, J.C Dorsainvil, Étienne Charlier, Jean Price-Mars and Arthur Holly. *La Revue indigene* had a six month run which was considered a success for the life of a publication in those hectic days.

Georges Petit launched *le Petit Impartial* in 1927 as an organ of *La Jeunesse Patriote Haitienne.* Born from discussion groups, their journals had brief tenures but they were powerful on reflecting new ideas and stirred the intelligence to life and brought the Haitian presidents and the U.S Occupation draconic press laws down on their necks. The writers, poets and scholars rejected old French cultural values and promoted Haitian ones and a truly Haitian literature that emphasized African heritage. The occupying Marines brought their racist attitudes with them and let it be known that no matter how light a mulatto anyone with an ounce of black blood was a black.

Max became a socialist, but unlike his friend, Jacques Roumain, never a Communist. He had no theoric Marxist formation, but he definitely favored socialism. He was a man of action and quite incapable of accepting a rigid party dictate. However, along with Jacques Roumain, he had been arrested, tried, and sentenced to prison for purportedly being a communist during an occupation red-hunt. After his trial, Hudicourt made clear that while he identified with the ideology's principles he was not personally a communist. A hunger strike and international attention won him and Roumain early releases from prison.

He continued to be an outspoken dissident against President Sténio Vincent; (1930-41) who, he felt, had betrayed Haiti's nationalist movement by allying with the United States after the Marines withdrew.

President Trujillo seated next to President Vincent and ambassador Lescot.

As leader of *La Reaction Democratique* in 1932, he edited their *Le Centre,* and, the following year, Hudicourt was arrested accused of disseminating communist ideology. Released from the National Prison one time he refused to give up his convict garb, called *rad makak* and startled his family returning home dressed as a convict. Usually, the government ordered his arresting officer to be Captain Lucien Scott ,his brother-in-law,.

In the late thirties, the world was distracted by the Spanish Civil war which pitted Generalissimo Francisco Franco's Fascist insurgents against the Republican government's loyalists on the eve of the Second World War. With Nazi Germany and Fascist Italy aiding Franco, leftists the world over sought to aid the Loyalists. The war drew writers especially. A voluntary force named the Abraham Lincoln Brigade was form by Americans and they fought. In Haiti as elsewhere the Catholic Church sided with Franco, and the radical left with the Loyalists.

In his book, **Dangerous Dossiers**, Herbert Mitgang, details the extraordinary campaign waged against America's greatest authors by FBI's zealot, Edgar J. Hoover .He secretly created intelligence dossiers from intrusive surveillance on writers, poets and even a famous economist, and not one was a communist. The FBI (U.S. Federal Bureau of Investigation) kept dossiers on American supporters of the Spanish loyalists whose side, for a time, was the Soviets' through the Communist International but the Comintern failed. The red-hunting spread to the Caribbean and South America and notably Haiti when the FBI was officially, during the war years, placed in charge of intelligence gathering. It was superseded after World War 11 by the CIA (Central Intelligence Agency).

When President Vincent decided to take the well worn authoritarian path in 1938, Hudicourt helped organize a large demonstration to which the authorities responded with severe repression. As protest leaders were rounded up and jailed, Hudicourt this time narrowly escaped arrest by fleeing to New York. He was tainted, but he was not one to enjoy the Byzantine discussions about the Leninist ways .The FBI thought otherwise and kept him under their gaze filling his dossier as a foreign red.

Chapter 19

Power and Protests

Political and social organs aimed at the liberation of the masses from the "avarice and discrimination of capitalist governments and foreign powers," during the Élie Lescot presidency, and editors were jailed.

When Max Hudicourt returned two years after Élie Lescot succeeded Vincent in the presidency, he was immediately put under police surveillance. In 1941 he had criticized a police chief while campaigning for a congressional seat. The result was a police attack, beating him, and Hudicourt was again exiled to the Dominican Republic and then New York. He returned in 1942 after negotiations and was allowed to print a daily socialist newspaper called *La Nation*. He financed the paper from his own funds, raised from a small Petionville movie house he co-owned.

Author Matthew J ,Smith in *"Red and Black in Haiti noted* Hudicourt's *La Nation* was the "leading voice of the Marxist Left and ultimately became the longest running Marxist paper in Haitian history. It significantly influenced the young intelligentsia and was widely circulated among literate urban works. Most articles gave considerable attention to the war, with special concern over the progress of the Red Army on the eastern front. Speeches from Latin American Marxists in Mexico, Argentina, and Cuba were translated and printed in their entirety. There were also a series of theoretical articles on socialism and culture and the role of the USSR in the struggle for autonomy in Algeria."

Smith writes, "Although its reportage was mainly devoted to international events *La Nation* covered local stories and often suffered as a result. In July 1943, the paper ran an article criticizing police chief Merceron's brother, who, in a drunken brawl, shot four bystanders. In response the police chief threatened to kill Hudicourt, before Lescot intervened. Following this incident the paper refrained from reporting government activities. This did not mean, however, that the directors of *La Nation* gave up their protest against the government. Hudicourt, for example, fearing that impending legislative elections in 1944 would provide an occasion for the government to extend its powers, continued to draw international attention to the administrations' failures. In a letter to Cordell Hull, he discussed these issues and pointed to the "share of responsibility" borne by the United States since the occupation in creating the current crisis in Haiti. It was thus the duty of the "guilty" U.S. government to intervene and force Lescot to respect the provisions of the Atlantic Charter.

"In March 1944, Hudicourt was named juridical counselor of the Haitian delegation sent to the Conference of International Workers Organizations in Philadelphia. Though suspicious of Lescot's intentions, Hudicourt saw it as an opportunity to work toward the improvement of the conditions of urban workers and accepted the post. During his absence, however, Lescot, beleaguered by the SHADA debacle and the threat it posed to his control, announced the extension of his term of office for seven years, a revision of the constitution, and the suspension of congressional elections until after the war. Hudicourt responded strongly by refusing to serve at the conference on behalf of Haiti and issued public statements to that effect in Philadelphia. Lescot was incensed. In his inaugural address on 15 May 1944, he referred to Hudicourt specifically by stating that the "injurious and malicious" campaign against the administration by young "pseudo-defenders of the proletariat" would not be tolerated. Lescot made good on this threat by issuing two decree laws in late May, stating that anyone given a foreign mission and refusing to fulfill it would be guilty of treason and liable to court-martial. The decrees were made retroactive for a year so that Hudicourt would be held accountable. Accordingly, the government revoked his passport and, under an extradition treaty with the United States, demanded his immediate return to Haiti. A month after Hudicourt left, *La Nation*, along with *Le Réveil*, was shut down by the government Lescot stating it was for "raising questions that sought to divide the citizens against each other," for "sowing hate and fomenting trouble," and for their attempt to "make Haiti a ground of disorders." The paper was also implicated in a sergeants' revolt against Lescot.

"With the assistance of the American Civil Liberties Union, Hudicourt secured refugee status from the U.S. government and left Philadelphia to settle in New York, where he remained in exile for the rest of the Lescot presidency. There he worked with another political exile, Henri Rosemond, building an underground network of radicals sympathetic to the Haitian cause and developing *L'Association Démocratique Haïtienne*. As in 1940, he was successful in gaining support from U.S. black intellectuals in Harlem. He wrote several pamphlets sponsored by *L'Association Democratique Haitienne* whose secretary was Lucas

Premice who had befriended Hudicourt. *"Haiti Faces tomorrow's Peace"* was published in Feb 18, 1945, with a foreward by Gene Weltfish of Columbia University's Department of Anthropology and translated from the French by Anita Delyn Weinstein. The pamphlet detailed the abuses of the Haitian government and U.S. policy in the country. Pessimistic as he was for his country's future Hudicourt used a quote from an American writer who said of Haitian history, "It will again be necessary to dip her pen in the sun and write in golden letters on the blue of the sky."

[In New York, Max was friends with Lucas Premice (father of the famous singer Josephine Mary Premice) who had been imprisoned in Guiana. He and a fellow prisoner to whom he was chained escaped and fled through the woods to friends that awaited them on the coast. On the third day of their journey, the other man died, and Lucas is said to have had to cut off the man's arm to free himself from the chains. He was brought to France, where he learned to cut fur for the couturiers. He eventually immigrated to New York in the early 1920s.]

Far removed from this event, Jacques Roumain conducted his diplomatic functions in Mexico in fine fashion. He represented Haiti at the First Inter-American Congress on Demography, and as founding secretary was instrumental in establishing the International Institute of Afro-American Studies, which included international luminaries Fernando Ortiz, Melville Herskovits, and Alain Locke. His tenure in Mexico marked a return to literary writing, and in late 1943 he completed a manuscript that would become his *chef d'oeuvre* and a hallmark of Caribbean literature, *Gouverneurs de la Rosée* (Masters of the Dew). His health, however, deteriorated rapidly during these years. The malaria he contracted during his incarceration, from which he never fully recovered, coupled with health problems related to alcoholism, weakened him. When Lescot extended his term of office and postponed legislative elections, Roumain considered challenging him and returned to Haiti on 7 August. Fellow communists, the numbers of which were growing among the youth during the final stages of the war, expected him to repudiate his allegiance to the government and seriously reorganize

President Sténio Vincent presiding over a luncheon at the Palace on Haiti's Independence Day, 1 January 1934. Foreign Minister Èlie Lescot is on Vincent's right with members of Garde d'Haiti High Command (mostly members of U.S. Marine Corps.)
(Courtesy U.S. National Archives)

President Lescot and staff leaving church service after investiture as president.

Haiti Faces Tomorrow's Peace

By MAX L. HUDICOURT

Director of the newspaper "La Nation"
Vice-President of the Inter-American Press Society

Translated from French by ANITA DLYN WEINSTEIN

Jacques Roumain

Lescot and the ladies

The Triumph

of

Fascism

or

THE HAITIAN-AMERICAN MUTUAL
RESPONSIBILITIES IN THE
HAITIAN AFFAIRS

BY

MAX L. HUDICOURT

COMITE DE LUTTE POUR UNE HAITI DEMOCRATIQUE
306 FULTON STREET   BROOKLYN 16, NEW YORK

As Haitian police and the FBI kept close watch on the faltering Haitian leftist movement, Hudicourt continued his political activity from exile in Harlem, New York. He attacked the Lescot government and US policy in the Caribbean and networked with other progressive intellectuals. His works from exile include "The Triumph of Fascism: Or the Haitian-American Mutual Responsibilities in Haitian Affairs" (1945). In New York, during the forties, he worked in the kitchen of the Plaza Hotel before he graduated to the Waldorf's. Then he opened a Haitian restaurant.

for having published a mimeographed bulletin reclaiming the freedom of elections for the Haitian people, was arrested, tortured, beaten, and judged by a military tribunal and condemned to six years of forced labor   Mr. Lavelanet, director of the newspaper "Le Peuple," for having asked for an augmentation of the salaries of air force soldiers holding the rank of private, was also arrested, judged in secret and condemned . . . Max Audain and Desrosier were shot.

During the same months, President Lescot, who claimed that we can only be saved by our powerful neighbor, said in his speech of October 17, 1945, that we must save ourselves.   In this same speech he announces that his Minister of Finance is in Washington where he is asking assistance in a "Five Year Plan."

Three years ago he professed to have already saved us by giving us the American Shada Company of Agriculture.   In a speech at Gonaves, after the failure of the said Company, he made the Company responsible for all our misfortunes and declared that its directors had deceived his government.

He confessed ignorance, a type of ignorance which is completely dishonest, for before the signing of the contract with the Shada Company, Mr. Burr-Reynaud and myself had predicted in public articles the inevitable failure of the enterprise.   These articles occasioned the suppression of the newspaper "Le Temps Nouveau."

And again, during this same month of October, the Health Service, which was directed by a Haitian doctor, was bestowed with the agreement of the United States Embassy to an American Doctor Griffits, sent here from New York by Clipper that October.

For eighteen years this service had been directed by American Military doctors during the time of the military occupation.   When the service was again entrusted to a

•

5

After Lescot was exiled amidst the popular revolution of 1946, Hudicourt returned to lead *Parti Socialist Populaire* (PSP)." Author Matthew J, Smith in *"Red and Black in Haiti"* writes, "In 1946 he (Max) was elected as the PSP's candidate to the Chamber of Deputies, becoming the only sitting socialist politician. He was part of a 1947 failed high-level delegation to the United States to secure the forgiveness of occupation-era loans and debts .Failure to meet these demands would force them to incite a national strike to overthrow the *Conseil Executif Militaire*. The young communists clearly felt they retained the command over the Port-au-Prince workers that they had in January. Though the prospect of a provisional government headed by renowned leftists was unlikely, it was sufficient to raise serious concern among the military government and U.S. officials."Smith continues, "But much had changed in the four months following the Lescot overthrow. The military apparatus to maintain social control and, more important, the urban workers responded more readily to the *noiriste* rhetoric of Fignolé and his associates than to the Marxism of the student leaders of the January revolt. "Not surprisingly", writes Smith, "the loss of the seats in the National Assembly intensified the battle between the *noiristes* and Marxists in the radical press. When Dumarsais Estimé, in an effort to gain support for his presidential campaign, sent out congratulatory cards to the new senators and deputies, Max Hudicourt refused to accept the gesture. In *La Nation*, he issued a bitter assault against Estimé. Calling himself "a militant socialist," Hudicourt castigated the "reactionary fascist" Estimé, whose political career had been rife with contradictions and vacillations." In return he was painted as anti- *noiristes and* in the end, through Estime, chosen as president by parliament, *noiristes* won.

In May of that year, Smith writes, "Hudicourt was found slumped at his desk with a gunshot wound to his chest and revolver in hand. His apparent suicide was a total surprise to his allies in the PSP. Theories abounded that he was assassinated by political opponents or US agents, but his close friends said his death was the coda to a severe month-long depression. A draft article for *La Nation* naming corrupt civil and military officials lay on his desk..

With Hudicourt's death, his collaborators continued to publish several editions of *La Nation*, in which they examined his death, questioning whether it was suicide or murder. But as happened in the history of newspapers of the past, *la Nation* died with Max Hudicourt.

Red & Black *in Haiti;Radicalism,conflict,and political change,1934-1957 by Matthew J.Smith;University North Carolina Press.* This well researched 2009 book is highly recommended as it fills an important chapter in Haitian history

Chapter 20

U.S. Marine Corps authors

The U.S. occupation of Haiti from 1915 to 1934, turned at least two U.S. Marines – Capt. John Houston Craige and Lt. Faustin Wirkus, into bestselling authors, a la "The Yellow Kids." Their books shed some light on the occupation but they were of the same genre of literature as their predecessors, exploiting voodoo and strange happenings in Haiti.

Craige published "Black Bagdad" in 1933 and "Cannibal Cousins" the following year. Both books were partly autobiographical. The titles alone brought instant condemnation from Haitians. Two cauliflower ears, a broken nose and a Mexican bullet in his hip were silent testimony to the fact that Craige was a man of action. Son of a well-known Philadelphia family, he ran away to sea at the age of 14. He was a cowboy, mule-skinner and Latin American revolutionary; a gold minder and a heavyweight boxing champion of France. As a captain in the U.S. Marine Corps and chief of police of Port-au-Prince, Craige had more knowledge of Haiti than the average Marine officer.

"One of my duties as police chief …was to arrest newspaper editors.One day…we pulled up in front of a small,one story wooden shack set a little way back from the street. Over the door was the sign, 'Imprimerie Chauvet' …inside were three or four desks covered with mounds of ink-smeared paper. At the largest desk sat a rotund young man dressedib baggy linen trousers and a sport-shirt with a wide, turned down collar,exposing an area of sunburned chest and powerful neck.His hair and eyes were light in color.He was almost blond. On the back of his head was a huge, white, felt sombrero and in his mouth was a big cigar. He looked a bit like the busts of the youthful Balzac and exuded an atmosphere of abounding vitality.

"This was Chauvet, member of a fine old family of the élite…with him was a smaller darker man, Duvigneaud, his partner, ana sparse, older Haitian, their assistant editor…

" Beside the Nouvelliste there were in Port-au-Prince two principal opposition papers…One of them was the 'Temps', headed by Mr.Charles Moravia. Moravia was a highly educated and accomplished gentleman.He was tall, dignified,light complexioned…His criticisms were well written,serious and well thoughtout. He annoyed the Occupation and the government as much as Chauvet, but in a different way.

"The third of the opposition editors was on Jolibois fils. Jolibois's paper was called the 'Courier Haitien'. He was small, vulgar and very black. Whereas Chauvet and Moravia were members of the elite, decidedly gentlemen in their ways, honorable according to their characteristically Haitian creed, Jolibois appeared to have no standard (He constantly attack the Occupation and was imprisoned so often a solitary confinement cell in the national penitentiary is still called the Jolibois-Ed) Haitian or other…there was a chanson that he did not wash frequently or extensively…on the other side of the fence there were two principal pro-government sheets, the Le Matin and the Essor. The Matin was edited by a very able, French appearing gentleman, named Clement Magloire. The Essor was edited by a remarkable Haitian, a Dr.Dorsainvil.* (Incorrect it was edited by Mr.Dorsainville,)

 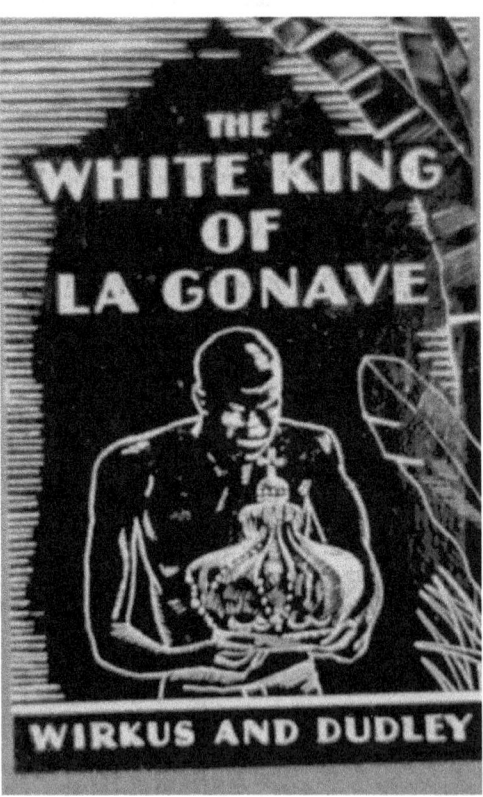

Wirkus authored "The White King of La Gonave," published in 1931, a book that smacks of the old colonial white superiority scenario, although the book, - co-authored by Taney Dudley, a woman writer who lived in Haiti and got to know Wirkus – is not unfavorable to Haitians. Its theme: A young Marine becomes King of the island in the bay off Port-au-Prince. With its publication, Wirkus' exploits became internationally famous and in Harpers in 1933 the famous magazine published his article, "The Black Pope of Voodoo"…In 1929, Col. Frederck May Wise wrote, "A Marine tells it to you."

Wirkus tells of his amorous adventure, first at Perodin and then at the village of Casale, which he spells Carzal. Polish soldiers members of Napoleon's expedition force to enforce slavery deserted and many ended up living the rest of their lives in Casale.

The Marine writes, "On one of my first visits to Carzal (sic) I met her. She was squatting, Haitian fashion, on the edge of the creek with a group of women of mixed colors doing the family wash. A brilliant bandanna was twisted around her blonde hair and her fair skin startlingly white by contrast with the brown and yellow woman around her. She was laughing And chattering in Creole. She didn't pay much attention to us, but I couldn't take my eyes off of her.

"After that I saw her on almost every visit I made to Carzal…I felt myself slipping. I knew it was not the thing to do. Marie seemed white, was white, but the fact remained that her mother was a rotund brown lady who did not know any too certainly who was Marie's father…She was a lovely child and I wanted very much to please her and make her happy.

"The nearest thing to the heart of a Haitian girl is shoes. Marie had never had a pair in her life. One day, sitting on the edge of the creek under the palm trees, she had told me of her lust for shoes. I had taken off my belt and measured her foot most exactly by a pencil mark from the end of the tongue of the buckle to the inner surface of the leather, and I promised that on my next trip to Port she would have her shoes.

"Rambling around Port-au-Prince… I walked straight into the nearest store and bought a pair of high-heeled blue linen slippers with embroidered flowers on them. They were lovely shoes, light-blue, with embroidery in darker blue and pink…

Lieutenant Wirkus goes on to visualize Marie' happiness when she receives the shoes but worries about an entanglement and finally sends one of his gendarmes at Arcahaie to Casale with the shoes. Marie has gone into the mountains to visit an aunt. The gendarme finds a tall Syrian pretending to be a good friend of Lieutenant Wirkus and takes delivery of the shoes.

"Weeks went by and one day I saw a tall, lithe figure straying through the streets of Arcahaie---Marie!

"I called and she came running…she saw me glance at her shoes… you did not come back, my friend—she said---and it is well you did not care but another did, my Syrian friend, he understood. He came to me one day and asked me if I was wild about the "blanc" lieutenant.

I said he had gone away. Then he reach under his coat, my Syrian, and gave me these wonderful slippers… and I have made 'marriage' with him…are you not glad for me?"

(It became a legend in Casale how the *blan* fell in love with Marie .)

Onetime newsman William B. Seabrook, in his book "*Magic Island*," gives a much better view of the U.S. occupation than either Craige or Wirkus. Seabrook had become city editor of the Augusta (Georgia) Chronicle at the age of 21. He quit and bummed around the world for a period then enlisted in the French army in 1915.In 1924, he returned to writing for Sunday newspapers, once saying of his career: "I have been searching for something that I have never found, and the search is somewhat complicated because I do not know what it is I am seeking. My writing, I think, is merely a by-product of that restless news." He spent time in the north Arabian desert and, eventually, arrived in Haiti where he spent 18 months. His book, published in 1929 – a time when a book on Haiti might have been expected to be skeptical, contemptuous and superior – is written with understanding and respect for the ancient moods and customs he encountered. Dr. Price-Mars objected to the word "*sauvagerie*" in Seabrook's descrpition of a woman's looks.

"*Black Haiti: A biography of Africa's Oldest Daughter*," by Blair Niles, is another noteworthy book of the period. Niles, as Seabrook, tried to be sympathetic to the Haitians but it also demonstrates that to sell a book about Haiti – or even a newspaper article – voodoo had to be exploited.

Garde d'Haiti by the United Marine Corps,1956 is an important book because it is written by the institute that for 19 years occupied Haiti.

"Occupation is distasteful to any people, and the Haitians were no exception. Their pride was hurt, and they were very sensitive over the conditions. The people were inclined to be hypercritical. Much of the antagonism was perhaps a cover-up for their true feelings. With some exceptions, the Haitians were not antagonistic to the Americans, but they were critical of the policies of the United States government. These criticisms were based on four main facts;
1. Uncertainity about the United States' intentions.
2. The incompetence of some of our representatives.
3. Failure to settle internal loans and to make a new loan.
4. arbitrary actions of both Marines and civilians."(p.38)

Serious work by foreigners

Life in a Haitian Valley
By Melville J.Herskovite, New York, 1937

Finally with Professor Herskovites, serious books, well researched appeared and were followed by Leyburn, Courlander and Deren.their approach was scientific and devoid of sensationalism. Herskovite meticulously examines life in the valley of Mirebalais.For students these books are important.

Tell my horse

By Zora Neale Hurston, Philadelphia,1938 and re-edited in 1967 and 1981.

Professor Leyburn ,in his bibliography of *The Haitian People* states, "*Tell My Horse* is a gaily written study of certain details of life in Jamaica and Haiti. Much of the detail is hearsay, some is inaccurate, but a great deal is carefully observed,"

Haiti Singing

By Harold Courlander the University of Carolina press 1939
 This is an extraordinary book that is such a pleasure to read.
An ethnologist with literary talent he writes, "In the hills of Haiti everyone sings and dances. Babies of three years dance Vodou and Pètro with their elders. Boys of seven are already master drummers under the teaching of their fathers, who learned from their own fathers. And old women weighed down by years and infirmities still dance Ibo with their shoulders.
" In Haiti everyone works. If they do not work they do not live. Most of them work very hard. But whether they work hard or not so hard, living is difficult and unbounteous…

The Haitian People

By James G Leyburn, Yale University Press,1941.

   Dr.Leyburn's thesis is that Haiti is divided not in classes but in castes. He was attacked by Dr. Jean Price Mars and despite provoking controversy the book is a serious, complete and deep analysis of the turbulent Haitian society before World War 11

Divine Horsemen
Voodoo Gods of Haiti

By Maya Deren, New York,1952.

The "Divine Horsemen" was published in 1952 but Deren spent time in Haiti during the forties after the inquisition against Vodou the "champagne des rejetes".Her description of her possession by lwa Ezulie is not only interesting to ethnolopists, but it is superb poetry.

Voodoo in Haiti
 By Alfred Métraux

This is masterwork of observation and description by one of the most distinguished anthropologists of the twentieth century. Alfred Métraux (1902–1963) has written a rich and lasting study of the lives and rituals of the Haitian *mambos* and adepts, and of the history and origins of their religion. It is an accurate and engaging account of one of the most fascinating and misunderstood cultures in the world. The author did much of his research in the Marbial Valley in the 1940s.

Chapter 21

Help thy Neighbor

Readers of *Le Nouvelliste*, Haiti's evening newspaper, learned the day it happened in 1930 that a terrible hurricane had befallen Santo Domingo. "Disaster In The Sister City," proclaimed *Le Nouvelliste's* headline. The first report from across the border said that half of Santo Domingo had been destroyed, 300 were known dead and 900 injured. The Haitian government organized the first relief, a truckload of drugs, accompanied by Haitian doctors and officers. It also made available a small army plane to fly Charles Moravia, publisher of *Le Temps* and one of the most able Haitian newsmen of the time, to Santo Domingo to cover the aftermath of the hurricane. He was one of the first foreign journalists to reach the scene. His eyewitness report of the disaster won worldwide attention as the Associated Press put his account on their wire service and it was published by AP's clients around the world. It was a graphic report of the burning of more than 800 dead, the stench invading the cockpit of the small plane as it arrived in Santo Domingo.

Haitians were moved to aid their neighbors. All available drugs were shipped immediately, followed by agricultural products that were brought to Port-au-Prince from the small farms surrounding the capital, extending as far southwest as Leogane. The relief supplies were assembled and taken to Santo Domingo on a Lykes Line ship, along with flour and other staples. Engineers followed with materials to repair roads and power lines. Gen. Rafael Leonidas Trujillo Molina, who had so recently made himself president, sent a letter and two successive telegrams of thanks to Haitian president Eugene Roy, and the organizations that had aided his country. Trujillo's effusive letter and telegrams were prominently displayed in Port-au-Prince newspapers.

Five years later, in 1935, a terrible flood ravaged the region surrounding Jeremie in southern Haiti. Floodwaters covered a wide area and untold numbers of people drowned, their bodies swept out to sea. Some put the casualties in the thousands. Hundred sought refuge on a bridge over a river, only to be washed out to sea when the bridge was swept away. The following day, ships in the area found the ocean filled with bodies being eaten by sharks. The U.S. Naval Base in nearby Guantanamo, Cuba, sent out ships, but found no survivors. Trujillo, in the neighboring Dominican Republic, sent relief supplies, in a form of payback for the assistance Haiti had provided five years earlier. But by 1937, his so-called "compassion" for the Haitians soured and thousands were massacred as part of Trujillo's effort to "purify" the Dominican race from blackness as he invented, a new acceptable color; "*indio obscuro.*"

The climate for journalists in the Dominican Republic during Trujillo's rule (1930-61) was the most inhospitable in the region. The press under the dictatorship of El Benefactor, as Trujillo was known, produced considerable amount of material, most of which was worthless, except to demonstrate how sycophantic learned men can become under such circumstances.

The biggest story of 1937 and of Trujillo's reign, apart from his assassination, took time to leak to the world: the massacre of thousands of Haitians, with the rivers running red with their blood.

It was a story to bring even more fame to Quentin Reynolds, then a journalist for Collier's magazine. He later recounted it this way:

"Editors, of course, are born, not made. A good editor has to have second sight. In 1937 we had such an editor at Collier's. His name was William Cherney and he had received his early training in the rough, hurly-burly of Denver newspaper wars. One afternoon he came to me with a short clipping from the New York Times. It was a UP (United Press) story of about six lines and it merely reported that there were rumors of fighting between soldiers of the Dominican Republic and Haitian farmers. The alleged fighting was at the Dominican Haitian border and some natives had limped into Port-au-Prince with stories that many of their compatriots had been killed.

"'There might be a story in this,'" Cherney said mildly. " 'Get a plane to Miami. From there you can fly to Santo Domingo. See Trujillo and go to Haiti and see Vincent (the Haitian president). Try to get where the trouble is supposed to be. You may find a story there.'"

"Apparently these are just rumors," 'I said.' "Maybe there's no story there at all."

"'That could be,'" Cherney said, shrugging his shoulders, " 'but it's worth a try. Besides, it's very cold here in New York. You'll find the weather down there nice. If there's no story there, we've only wasted a week or so of your time. I guess we can stand that.'"

"So that night I caught a plane to Miami and woke up wondering who in hell Trujillo was. Who was Vincent? I had no idea. Since I had a couple of hours to kill in Miami, I went to the morgue of The Miami Herald. Under Trujillo I found Rafael Trujillo, President of Santo Domingo; under Vincent, I got Stenio Vincent, President of Haiti. Then I went to Santo Domingo and the next day found myself lunching with His Excellency, President Rafael Trujillo.

"It was a very good meal, which began with cocktails and ended with Lanson, 1928, as good a champagne as you'll find in a year of travel. President Trujillo was a handsome, friendly man with copper skin and twinkling eyes. He drank a mighty good glass of wine, too. He reminded me a lot of Ernst Roehm, with his hail fellow well met attitude. I asked him about those rumors of trouble at the border. He nodded understandingly and discussed them with what appeared to be great frankness.

"'Yes, it is true,' he sighed. 'A few Haitian farmers crossed the border up north and tried to steal some goats and cattle from our farmers. There was a fight – very regrettable – and several were killed on both sides. Ordinarily, we have only one judge up there in the north. I immediately sent others to adjudicate the case and see what justice was done. The proceedings are quite open" – he smiled disarmingly – "to representatives of Haiti.'"

"The luncheon broke up in a very friendly atmosphere, and you felt that it only needed someone to start singing 'For He's a Jolly Good Fellow,' to make it complete. I had just come from Germany and this reminded me very much of the Bierabende Putzi Hanfstaengl used to hold for the American press. The atmosphere was so heavy with friendliness that it oppressed you and stuck in your throat. So I left and went to Haiti and two days later stood in the Justinian hospital at Cap-Haitien. The hospital was bulging with patients and virtually all of them were suffering from knife and machete wounds.

"Dr. Anthony Leveque was in charge. 'Two weeks ago we had six patients here in the hospital. Two had malaria, three had skin infections. Now? Count them. Something like four hundred, nearly all with bad wounds. There are many times this number in first-aid camps we have established near the border. They were all wounded by Trujillo's soldiers.

" 'Can you believe their stories?'" I asked.

" 'Many of these men and women are going to die,'" he said, throwing me a look of contempt. 'They know it. They have received the last rites from Father Emil Robert and from our Bishop Jean-Marie Jan. They would not lie.'"

"So I talked to them and they told me then, of the things that had happened –things which Bert Hicks discussed in this book (*Blood in The Streets*). They told me that Trujillo had ordered the massacre of all Haitians who were in Dominican territory. The Haitians were not there illegally. Each year thousands of them went across the border to cut the sugar cane."

Reynolds later wrote the foreward to "*Blood in the Streets,*" by Albert C. Hicks, published in 1946. In his introduction, Reynolds notes that "Hicks decided to investigate Trujillo, fact and legend, after listening to and examining lots of terrifying one-sided evidence against the dictator. A good newspaperman and reporter, he maintained a healthy and objective suspicion about Trujillo until he had collected considerable first-hand stuff. He interviewed friends and enemies of Trujillo in Puerto Rico, Haiti and the United Sates, and elsewhere. In a short time he became known, to Trujillo's Gestapo. And he finally decided that he couldn't be objective about Trujillo any longer.

"…Trujillo has been in the driver's seat down there for more than fifteen years. Maybe this book will make his seat less secure," Reynolds said, likening the Caribbean caudillo to Hitler.

BLOOD in the STREETS
The Life and Rule of TRUJILLO
by ALBERT C. HICKS

DOMINICAN DICTATOR

Introduction by Quentin Reynolds

Trujillo was to last another 15 years. The book? It had no noticeable effect. The total dead in the 1937 massacre, according to Hicks, was closer to 20,000 than 15,000.

As the publisher of the English-language Haiti Sun, which also published a column in Creole, and resident correspondent in Hispaniola for Associated Press, The New York Times, NBC and Time-Life magazines, I became interested in the Dominican Republic in the early

1950s. My first close encounter with Trujillo was on the border at Belladére and Elias Pinas in February 1951. I was at the first meeting in 14 years between the two neighboring presidents. Some of the news people invited to accompany Haitian President Paul Magloire made the mistake of trying to ask Trujillo questions as he descended the stairs in the government building in which the 371-page anti-Communist peace treaty was signed. Before he reached the bottom of the stairs, he issued orders for the nosy news people to be excluded from the party. They were literally shown the door and departed for Port-au-Prince.

Luckily, I was not with this group and managed to remain talking and dancing the meringue next to El Jefe with the daughter of a Dominican officer at the Elias Pina garrison while eavesdropping on his conversation. I agreed with Quentin Reynolds description of the Generalissimo; he was a first class actor as are most dictators.

Local stringers (reporters) for foreign publications in Ciudad Trujillo (as Santo Domingo was renamed by Trujillo) were expected to file only government handouts and other innocuous news. As a result, I often received news items in Haiti from travelers arriving from the Dominican Republic. It was impossible to get the Trujillo government, including the resident ambassador in Haiti, to confirm or deny any news items. Most of the anti-Trujillo sources proved reliable but they had to be extremely cautious and given time to cover their tracks because the Dominican intelligence network headed by Johnny Abbes, had spies throughout the hemisphere.

One case involved a Spanish exile working for a pharmaceutical company in Mexico who boarded a pan American Airways flight for Ciudad Trujillo but never officially arrived. In this case, airline sources were willing to talk and gave a first hand account of how the man had been spirited from the plane on arrival in the Dominican Republic, never to be seen again. The Dominican officials were correct; he had not passed through immigration so he had not officially arrived. Among the other disappearances I was to investigate journalistically was that of the Basque exile, Prof. Jesus Galindez, who was kidnapped in Manhattan in 1956. Because he was writing his thesis on Trujillo whose secretary he had once been.

Francis "Bud" Colegrove, a correspondent for Scripps-Howard newspapers was the victim in the single most famous incident involving a newsman under Trujillo. He had written a particularly critical series of stories on Trujillo in 1959, and was in the Dominican Republic on the scent of a new story. Colegrove was sitting in the front seat of a taxi that sideswiped a parked truck with its lights out at night. Colegrove was not killed, but half his head was shaved off. He lived for a time in a vegetative state, finally recovering enough to work on the newspaper copy desk. Many newsman suspected it was an "arranged" accident.

I was reminded of it a year later as I sped over the lonely highway – usually with no traffic in the late evening hours – between Ciudad Trujillo and Jimani. when I nearly crashed into a sugar train left parked without lights on the strip of highway near Barahona.

I had covered the gigantic loyalty parade (Time: March 7, 1960) Trujillo had ordered after uncovering a so-called assassination plot the previous January for which more than a hundred had been arrested. Thousands upon thousands of Dominicans were forced to march past and salute Trujillo, seated in a special stand erected in Avenida George Washington. The theme: "Trujillo for President in 1962." The image of him seated in an armchair under a canopy sipping cognac and waving a limp hand reminded me of ancient Rome. It was to be the last such compulsory "Love el Jefe" parade.

The trips back and forth from Haiti were more frequent after the abortive June 14, 1959, invasion from Cuba. The execution of prisoners made it a turbulent year. Opposition to El Jefe became more active and daring. Finally, the Church entered the fray. Some Dominicans shot their way into asylum in Latin America embassies, causing further embarrassment. Haiti was also providing increased news, as Francois "Papa Doc" Duvalier was well on the way to establishing his own dictatorship.

After 1957, any foreign correspondent arriving in the Dominican Republic did so under one of the world's most tightly controlled dictatorships. From the moment he stepped off the plane, he was under the scrutiny of the military Intelligence Service (SIM), headed by Johnny Abbes Garcia. As he entered the immigration at the airport, the journalist was told to turn right and read a notice about carrying his passport while in the Dominican Republic. As he did so, he was well aware he was being secretly photographed.

SIM agents were everywhere, and even those who were not agents were suspected of being so. The tall, uniformed doorman, whose job it was to solicit customers at the airport, was believed to be an agent. He was not. The taxi driver was an informer or possibly a Calie (a government spy and thug) who would have to report his movements to Abbes. And Abbes himself was a communications expert who had the country completely wired. Newsmen took for granted their room and the telephone in it were bugged. Most aware journalists were continually flushing the toilet as conversations were held in the bathroom. Fortunately, Ciudad Trujillo had a good water supply. Notes also were regularly flushed down the toilet.

Those foreign newsmen who had read up on Trujillo's fiefdom and were aware of the many horror stories from exiles, did not approach an assignment to the country in a relaxed manner. Such was the paranoia that infected the foreign newsman, that he often made himself unapproachable. He suspected anyone who approached him of being an agent provocateur or just plain crazy, as no one in their right mind would be caught talking to a foreign journalist. It made reporting a difficult task. Abbes had such control that he dispensed with any outward signs of censorship or heavy-handedness. But newsmen took for granted the authorities were reading all their cables.

Those foreign correspondents who lingered too long in Ciudad Trujillo and began to establish sources and contacts were encouraged to leave. Such was the case of Edward (Ned) Burkes of the New York Times. He was reporting in the Dominican Republic in 1960, extending his stay to more than a month, much longer than the usual week-long visit of most foreign journalists, and too long for Trujillo. One day he received a summons that he was being sued by a Trujillo partisan for a large amount of money for slandering the man in one of his articles. He was given the choice of leaving or face Trujillo justice in court. His paper ordered him to leave.

In the first issue of *Le Manifeste*, April 4, 1941, Exilien Heurtelou, tongue in cheek, advises the Haitians on how to be a journalist: "Fill your columns with obituaries, compose lives of heroes of which you will narrate, in your own style, the achievements ornate with candles, myrtles, weepers, funeral hymns; in the foreign section, pile up all that you can find that is innocuous; be the echo of tales about our interesting bucolic maidens; in prose or in verse speak of Philomene and of the humming bird with the green, iridescent wings; dare, sometimes, some chronicles of yesteryears. Good! Very Good! You are a true journalist. But, the interests of the country, politics? Shhhh... You have not been appointed for that; the time has not yet come." (Castera P. 81.)

Publishing houses that would publish books were born in the post-Duvalier period in the late 20th century. Prior to Henri Deschamps publishing Papa Doc et les Tontons Makouts in 1986, a writer published and sold his own book. It also had become the custom for a writer to plead with the owner of a newspaper – and in some cases even pay – to have his essays, criticism or poems publish. To be noticed, a would-be politican had to publish or perish. One editor had a three-drawer desk into which the article of a writer would be placed. If the editor placed it in the lowest drawer there was little chanced of it appearing in the pages of the paper. Shelved in the other drawers, gave it a chance to see day light.

As late as the 1950s there were only three printing presses available to revues or magazines. They had to pay usually in advance to job-print at *Le Matin, Le Nouvelliste* or *Haiti-Journal* and depended on the politics and good humor of the publisher. The government's *L'Imprimerie de L'Etat* published, *Le Moniteur*, in which all official decrees were printed. Into the late 1950s Georges Petit's *Independence* newspaper was handset in type while the dailies used a linotype machine and flatbed printing presses. His son launched a Kreyol newspaper *Le Patriote*.

Vincent had launched his daily Haiti –Journal which died in the sixties and President Magloire *le National.* It disappeared when he flew off to New York exile. Duvalier, through military court, ended the *Haiti Mirror*, and his gunmen used a grenade to silence the small printing shop of Le Patriote. Veteran fighter Georges Petit's long career was ended, and he went to jail for the last time. *Le Nouveau Monde* became the Duvalier daily.

JOURNALISM is not dead

Once he got the story, the most frustrating thing for the foreign newsman was how to get it to his paper. At the beginning it was a simple matter of getting on a horse, or a boat, and sailing home with the story. The most able correspondent was often the best horseman. In France, a system of semaphore telegraph stations were set up about ten miles apart and preferably the wooden station was built on a hill and used wooden cut out of letters that were moveable. Each station was equipped with a telescope and the message was replayed across the country in this slow fashion at the end of the 18th century. Then l'Agence Havas, the first such news service scooped the government by simply using its own telescope to read the government messages.

Much later when communication was established by Morse Code, the telegraph, they sometimes relied on their local man who was a reporter for a local newspaper, "stringer" was his title. Le Matin had a technician who copied the Associated Press wire that was in Morse Code to be shared with customers around the world.

Typewriter copy went to a cable station. In two competing cable offices, RCA Cable and ALL America Cable an employee punched out the ribbon and sent the cable on to the recipient. West Indies Telephone Company also linked Haiti by telephone to the outside world during day light hours. A t night Haiti was closed to the exterior.

The government, under Martial law, could order all communication cut and applied censorship on all out-going traffic. An easy procedure. Journalists considering it their right to report the news broke censorship in a variety of ways, while governments accused them of breaking the law. (The Duvalier regime ordered all private Ham Radios to be placed in Police hands.)

Communications: from smoke signals to the Pentium chip then there is the Optic fiber which opens a new communications highway. The digital age has made it harder for dictators to exist as they can no longer hide their crimes behind censorships or even their illicit bank accounts of the people's money but of course as corruption became rife, they find other means to stash ill-gotten funds.

Chapter 22

Have Pen will travel: the Travel Writers

Haiti – exotic, mysterious and accessible – was made to order for the rising tide of sensational journalism and travel writers. Frederick Douglass, the great American black abolitionist, who was to become the top U.S. diplomat in Haiti at the end of the 19th century, did what he could to inform arriving correspondents about Haiti. But it apparently did little good; the kind of information he provided was not what sensationalism seeking reporters were looking for. One example comes from Frederick Ober in his 1893 travel book entitled *"In the Wake of Columbus."* In it, he reports that cannibalism was widely practiced in Haiti and recommended that the country should be saved from sliding into barbarism. Spencer St. John, a British diplomat, provided the primer on voodoo for sensationalism-seeking journalists in his *"Haiti or the Black Republic,"* published in 1884. It became the briefing book of the period on voodoo and set the tone for many books to follow. *"Where Black Rules White,"* by correspondent of the Daily Express, Hesketh Prichard, published in New York in 1900 is arrogant and at times as outrageous as that of Sir Spencer.

As a journalist he observes the Haitian press of the day, "If I were condemned to write down the names of all the newspapers of Hayti, past and present, I would have to spend a considerable amount of time upon the task. The reason of their multiplicity is not on account of any great demand for news…but because from a number of causes the journals of the daily press are apt to be short –lived.

"Whenever there is a revolution each party, each powerful leader, must perforce have an organ through which he may address the public generally and the inhabitants of Port-au-Prince in particular. So each political commotion brings in its train a crop of newspapers, proclamations, pamphlets - call them what you will—whose average length of life is limited to half-a-dozen issues…

"These journals have a humor of their own for the European reader. They are conducted by Haytian journalists whose style appears to lend themselves to a rather bombastic tone, and whose grasp upon foreign affairs is superlatively French…

…it must be difficult to preserve freedom of utterance when, at the first symptom of independence, the enterprising editor is dragged off to prison…At the present time Port-au-Prince possesses two papers '*Le Soir*' and '*Le Nouvelliste*' whose views upon local questions are absolutely colorless.. Their content includes telegrams from French sources, an article by a leading Haytian, and a patchwork of utterly unimportant local news."(P. 225-227.)

More travel writers

" For his own purpose, as well as to act as an independent newspaper correspondent, the author left New York on the 1st day of February in the Steamer Tybee, the only steam-vessel that keeps up communication between the Republic of St. Domingo and the United States."

Samuel Hazard was not only to report but also to turn his trip into a book: *Santo Domingo: Past & Present with a glance at Haiti*," published in 1873 by Harper & Brothers.

This tradition of travel writer produced more than a score of books on the island during the early part of the 20th century. They included: "*Combing the Caribbees*" by Harry I. Foster, published in 1929 by The Bodley Head Ltd ; "*Roaming Through the West Indies*" by Harry A. Franck, published in 1921 by the Century Co; The "*White Elephants in the Caribbean*," by Henry Albert Phillips, published in 1936 by Robert M. McBride and Co.; and "*Caribbean Treasure*" by Ivan T. Sanderson, published in 1940 by Hamish Hamilton.

Harry Franck who wrote about his visit to Haiti in 1919 began his book with a "forewarning", "The following pages do not pretend to "cover" the West Indies (Caribbean). They are made up of the random pickings of an eight month tour of the Antilles." And his pickings often have a racial tone. Another travel book was,"*Crossroads of the Caribbean Sea*, by Hendrik de leeuw. And *Democracy and Empire in the Caribbean* by Paul Blanshard (1947) published by the Macmillan Company. A series of pulp fiction by Hugh B, Cave centered on Haiti were enjoyable reading about the highroad to adventure.

Luckily for students and scholars these travel books were followed by more serious authors, anthropologists and sociological researchers.

British authors specialized in travel books and *The Traveler's Tree*; A Journal though the Caribbean Island (1945) is a classic. It was followed by *Bonjour blanc, a journey through Haiti'* (Ian Thomson, 2004). It is one of the best written travel books about Haiti. The 20 chapters of the book are both entertaining and informative. Mark Kurlansky's "*White man in a tree*" is a worthy and enjoyable read, even today.

The list of newspapers that published information about the rebellion include:

Bahama Gazette (Nassau) 1789-1804.

Baltimore Daily Repository, 1791-1793.

Baltimore Federal Gazette, 1796-1804.

Baltimore Federal Intelligencer, 1794-1795.

Boston Gazette, 1789-1802.

Boston Independent Chronicle, 1789-1804

Boston Price-Current, 1795-1798.

Bulletin Officiel de Saint-Domingue (Le Cap Francais, 1791-1804)

Charleston City Gazette 1789-1804

Charleston Times, 1800-1804

Cornwall Chronicle (Montego Bay, Jamaica),1796-1798.

Le Courier de L'Amerique (Philadelphia), 1792-1793.

Courier Francais (Philadelphia), 1794-1798.

L'Etoile Americaine (Philadelphia),1794.

Gazette National, ou Le Moniteur Universal (Paris) 1789-1804

Gazette Officielle de Saint-Domingue (Le Cap Francais),1789-1804

Journal des Revolutions (New York), 1793.

Maryland Journal and Baltimore Advertiser, 1789-1797

Minerva and Mercantile Evening Advestiser (New York),1796-1797.

Mirror of the Times and General Advertiser (Wilmington, Del.), 1799-1804.

Moniteur de la Louisiane (New Orleans,)1794-1804.

Newport Mercury, 1789-1804.

New York Daily Gazette, 1789-1795.

New York Evening Post, 1794-1795, 1801-1804.

Le Patriote Francois (Paris),1789-1804.

Philadelphia Aurora, 1794-1804.

Philedelphia General Advertiser, 1790-1794.

Providence Gazette and Country Journal, 1789-1804

St. George's Chronicle and Grenada Gazette, 1798-1799.

Salem Gazette, 1790-1804.State Gazette of South Carolina (Charleston, 1